D0616720

i'm a freaking GENIUS

Why Don't I Have More Money?

i'm a freaking GENIUS

Why Don't I Have More Money?

HELPING SMALL BUSINESS OWNERS

become not-so-small business owners.

MIKE CAMPION

Published by Advantage, Charleston, South Carolina.
Member of Advantage Media Group.

ADVANTAGE is a registered trademark and the Advantage colophon is a trademark of Advantage Media Group, Inc.
Printed in the United States of America.

ISBN: 978-159932-562-0
LCCN: 2015932175

Book design by George Stevens.

This publication is designed to provide accurate and authoritative information in regard to the subject matter covered. It is sold with the understanding that the publisher is not engaged in rendering legal, accounting, or other professional services. If legal advice or other expert assistance is required, the services of a competent professional person should be sought.

Advantage Media Group is proud to be a part of the Tree Neutral® program. Tree Neutral offsets the number of trees consumed in the production and printing of this book by taking proactive steps such as planting trees in direct proportion to the number of trees used to print books. To learn more about Tree Neutral, please visit **www.treeneutral.com**. To learn more about Advantage's commitment to being a responsible steward of the environment, please visit **www.advantagefamily.com/green**

To my beautiful bride, Nathalie: without you, I suck.

TABLE OF CONTENTS

Part Three: Let's Talk about People

Introduction

"Ordinarily he was insane, but he had lucid moments when he was merely stupid."

—Heinrich Heine,
German critic and poet

"People think it must be fun to be a supergenius, but they don't realize how hard it is to put up with all the idiots in the world."

—Calvin, ***Calvin and Hobbes***

I *Am a Freaking Genius: Why Don't I Have More Money?* Did that cause your inner voice to say "Self, I must get my hands on this book and read every word this man has ever written about anything," or some variation thereof? If so, you, sir (or ma'am) are in the right place, not to mention you are quite possibly my new best friend.

You have the brains, the skill, and the savvy, but your bank account does not reflect properly what a rock star you are and, quite frankly, you are sick of it. I have owned my own businesses since I was 22. Now that I am an old man of 40, and I can assure you I spent years toiling, struggling, working, and not getting the results I knew I should be getting. Don't get me wrong; I had success but not at the level that I could or should have had.

It took me nearly 20 years of working at it and learning the hard way to figure this whole business thing out: two steps forward and one step back—and I am still learning! If I had a book like this as a young man, I could have cut that time by two thirds and saved years of frustration. Looking back, I had 80 percent of it right; I was just missing a couple of key ingredients that kept me from being the success I knew I could be. If any of this is striking a chord with you, then buckle up. It's gonna be an exciting ride. If not, you might just be dead inside.

Before we move on, some questions might be rolling around your head, such as What on God's green earth does that title mean? Why should I read such a ridiculously titled book? Does this guy even know what he is talking about? This looks long and boring. Shouldn't I be watching TV right now?

Allow me to retort…

1. QUESTION

What on God's green earth does that title mean?

ANSWER:

I wish I had some high-power story about how I spent a fortune on market research and captured a million monkeys banging away on a million typewriters, day and night, seven days a week, to come up with the title. Truth be told, it sprang out of a conversation my super hot wife (the one from the acknowledgments page) and I were having one fine morning, while discussing business owner angst. I was droning on about how tough it is during the beginning stages of business, and how, when I was a young business owner, I thought I was smarter, stronger, and better than the mere mortals who surrounded me. But I never felt I had "arrived" in terms of money and my financial future. In her infinite wisdom, my wife blurted out, "I'm a freaking genius. Why don't I have more money?" I immediately fell in love with her all over again, and this book was born. Feel free to send her many gifts and letters of adoration.

PS: *(PS in the middle of an introduction? Is that even legal?)* If you read or even skim this book, you are going to realize in short order that I am not a real author. I'm just a regular guy with far better than average looks, who worked hard, made some money, and is arrogant enough to think he might be able to save some premature hair loss for a few of you out there. I'd like to think I can put you on the fast track to move your business into the million- or multimillion-dollar universe. Consider yourself warned.

---

2. QUESTION

Why should I read such a ridiculously titled book?

ANSWER

First of all, "ridiculously titled" seems a little harsh, but let's all just take a couple of deep breaths and move on.

Option #1: You are a guy or gal who shelled out 20 bucks for my book in hopes of a couple of tidbits that can make your life and business better, faster, easier. In that case, well done! You are in the right place, and I owe you a beer next time you are in town.

Option #2: You are an individual who has a business doing less than $1M in annual income, and you have a white-hot burning desire to grow that bad boy but feel you are never going to make it. Now we are talking! Our time together can save years of frustration, confusion, and a general bashing-your-head-into-a-wall type of scenario. In this case, you owe me a beer next time you are in town!

Option #3: You are my mom, reading one of the dozens of copies of this book you bought, and you are very proud of your little boy. In that case: hi, Mom!

3. QUESTION:

Does this guy even know what he is talking about?

SHORT ANSWER: YES.

LONG BORING ANSWER: STILL, YES.

I am not a Harvard graduate, but I am a proud alumni of Washington High School (Go Rams!), and that's about it for the whole "formal education" scene. After high school I attended—and I use that term loosely—one of our city's finest—I use that term quite loosely as well—community colleges for about 12 minutes. I realized it was chock full of liberal, anti-wealth, anti-business, anti-God Philistines, whom I didn't find intelligent or engaging at all. I dropped out and fooled around, waiting tables and working odd jobs until I got my first big-boy adult job as a car salesman. Car salesman? How did that happen?

Let's back up. I was raised to believe a couple of things that weren't all that helpful:

- **Not-so-helpful belief #1:** If I didn't have a college education, I couldn't get a job making any real money and I would end up turning wrenches and/or mowing lawns for a living. Let me be clear. I am a big fan of education. I have since invested tens of thousands of dollars—and continue to do so—by way of courses, seminars, books, CDs, mastermind groups, coaching, mentors, and the like, and recommend a posture of lifetime learning to all who will listen. That said, I am not a fan of dogmatic beliefs such as "If you don't go to college, you will never make any money."
- **Not-so-helpful belief #2:** I was raised poor, quite poor. My mom, who was just about the best mom a guy could ask for (hi, Mom!), worked her tail off as a single mother to put food on the table. That said, I developed a mentality that the rich were rich because they were born that way, and us poor were poor, and we would likely die that way. Since I didn't really know any "rich" people, I had no frame of reference and didn't realize until I was about 21 years of age that I could change my future in the greatest country on earth.
- **Not-so-helpful belief #3:** I figured I was just a kid whose only overhead was a Taco Bell addiction, and

> that since I saw real-life adults with wives, kids, and mortgages working as car salespeople, I could probably make a living selling cars, as a single guy. If you ever want a great story, ask about my interview at the first car dealership I worked at.

Now, you might be thinking, "A college dropout car salesman who says I can trust him… sounds fishy…" I know, I know. Just stick with me for another page or two.

After selling cars for a couple of years, and getting pretty good at it, I got married, celebrated my twenty-second birthday, and promptly went insane with the unshakable need to become a business owner. I decided to risk everything I had—which wasn't much, although it seemed like a lot at the time—to buy a business.

Long story short, I was not born rich, privileged, especially educated, or particularly gifted (aside from my striking good looks, of course), but I've managed to build, buy, and sell multiple businesses over the last 18 years. Two of them sold in the last three years for seven and six figures, respectively. It's okay. You can admit it. You're impressed I used the word respectively. Honestly, so am I. Do I have all the answers, the ten easy steps to become a rock-star millionaire over the next seven days, working only three hours a week? No. That's a sucker bet. Sorry to be the one to tell you.

PS: Santa is not real.

I am a guy with a ton of experience who has made more than his share of mistakes. I'm still passionate about business and want to help you, dear reader, make different mistakes from the ones I made. I want to help you achieve your goals faster, with way less brain damage and drama than I endured.

QUESTION

This looks long and boring. Shouldn't I be watching TV right now?

SHORT ANSWER

Depends on what's on TV. Is it football?

NOT-SO-SHORT ANSWER

There are a ton of actionable items in this book you can use today that are born out of doing things the hard way. I discovered a couple of life and business hacks along the way that you absolutely can use to change your life and force your business to serve you, instead of you being a slave to your business. You will find this book to be many things: boorish, poorly written, mildly offensive, outrageous, but definitely not stuffy, hard to understand, or impractical.

As a matter of fact, if you don't get at least ten times the value out of this book that you paid, come find me on the street, at Starbucks or a speaking engagement, hand me the book, tell me it was a total waste of your time, and I will give you $20 out of my pocket, assuming I have the money on me. If I don't, I will scribble a very official IOU on the closest napkin, tee shirt, or forearm, which you can readily exchange with my cash-carrying wife for said $20. Hope that helps.

I know we are still at the introduction and the getting-to-know-each-other phase, but I want to jump in and give you some actionable stuff right now. When I first started in business as the proud owner of a Service Master commercial cleaning business, I worked hard to be "professional." I was young, had a baby face, no credentials, no education, and wanted to look and feel like I "belonged," as if I were old enough to have a serious, professional business. I didn't realize at the time that I was missing out, and my customers and employees were missing out on the real me without the pretense or the mask. Turns out, that is what people really want! Luckily, all it took was a bat to the side of the head, by way of divorce, to get my attention and help me straighten myself out.

Side note: if you ever have the opportunity to get a divorce, pass!

My divorce was absolutely, irrefutably, amazingly debilitating. I didn't want to get dressed or leave the house, much less go to my business. Unfortunately (fortunately?) for me, the judge had different ideas and decreed that I would pay hundreds of thousands of dollars I didn't have immediately, along with thousands of dollars monthly. So, if I didn't want to end up in jail, making money was not an optional endeavor. As tempted as I am to rant, let's just say that I needed to earn around $80K annually just to pay my taxes and make my court-ordered payments and live at the poverty line. Anything over that went to my hundreds of thousands of dollars of court-ordered debt. Dark days, dear reader, dark days.

Okay, are you sufficiently depressed? Good. Let's turn a corner. I did go to work, but I couldn't bring myself to continue to present my professional facade to my employees, friends, and customers. I actually started a new company and decided that I wasn't able to waste any precious time, energy, or focus on "being professional."

I worked it out in my head and decided that I was going to be me, full on, 100 percent, through and through me. Instead of painting our new office walls grey like the old ones, we painted them red and tan. Instead of our old name, Del Riko Custom Fabric Design and Manufacturing—it hurts my fingers just to type such boring drivel—we went with Killer Shade. Instead of putting "CEO, President, King of the Universe," or some other pretentious title on my card, I dubbed myself "Janitor." Trust me fellas, the ladies loved it. I have dozens of examples, but you get the idea.

We dealt with architects, general contractors, and city planner types, who were not best known for their keen senses of humor. I figured 90 percent of them would laugh at, scoff at, and otherwise poo-poo my new identity, but I had high hopes the 10 percent of loyal leftovers would be enough for me to pay my bills.

I was wrong.

Ninety percent absolutely loved it, and 10 percent didn't care for the new and improved me, which was no worry, because I didn't particularly care for them. It wasn't limited to customers either. Employees, vendors, banks, and the community all wanted to be a part of our vibe. The response was overwhelmingly positive. There is a ton more about this in the chapter on core values because it is so key, but this should give you enough of a taste of who I am to help you to decide whether to keep this book and read it cover to cover, or give it to your 12-year-old so maybe he/she can finally get off his/her lazy butt and start bringing home some bacon!

Fast forward to today. I sold my last business, had money, and got bored. Tired of the buildings, the employees, the inventory, the payrolls, and the government regulations, I am fueling my passion by spending time helping the entrepreneurs I like, respect, and have fun with, which is exactly where this book comes in.

Part One

LET'S TALK ABOUT YOUR FAVORITE SUBJECT—YOU!

"How wonderful it is that nobody need wait a single moment before beginning to change the world."

—Anne Frank

"Success is walking from failure to failure with no loss of enthusiasm."

—Winston Churchill

Chapter 1

STOP READING ALREADY AND DO SOMETHING!

"It's not that I'm so smart; it's just that I stay with problems longer."

—Albert Einstein

"Vision without execution is hallucination."

—Henry Ford

I may have overreacted with the whole "Stop Reading" chapter title. Read chapter 1, then stop reading and do something. Maybe a nap… But after that, definitely come back and finish reading.

The reason this is the first chapter of the book is that this concept is foundational! If you get this chapter, own it, emblazon it across your chest in neon green, and make it a part of your life. Even if this is all you get out of this book, you still have gotten your time and money's worth. So ingest some caffeine and let's dive in!

A poor plan with excellent execution will kick butt over the "perfect plan" with no execution—every time! (Spoiler alert: perfect plans are about as easy to come by as unicorns.)

No matter how good this book is—and it's awesome—if you don't take these ideas and do something, it's not gonna happen. Nothing is going to work until you do! I learned in a Bible study discussion one day, long, long ago, that maturity is the gap between what you know and what you do.

To put it another way, you are better off not knowing a ton but doing what you do know well than having an ocean of knowledge at your disposal and not doing a dang thing.

Think about that for a second. Based on that definition, you can know very little and still be mature, as long as you *do what you know*. On the other hand, if you have a ton of knowledge—which we all seem to acquire as we grow older—attend more seminars, take more training, read more books, and so on, your knowledge grows much faster than your ability to implement it. This creates a large gap between what you know and what you put into practice. That spells immaturity. My fear in writing a book is that I will merely add more to your to-do list without any action or implementation.

Before we go any further, let me warn/assure/guarantee/be absolutely clear that if you do the things in this book, you will get results. If you merely read, nod, and smile at how swell these ideas are and how fantastic this author guy is, yet do nothing, you will get exactly the same results you have always gotten.

You will have more success implementing an adequate plan than ignoring the "perfect" plan. So please, before you continue, commit to taking two or three ideas from this book and translating them into action *today*. This leads us right into the next piece of this puzzle.

Massive immediate action tends to produce massive and immediate energy and momentum! When confronted with a good idea, we can choose to hem and haw, scratch our heads, Google it, debate whether or not it will work, ask a friend, do some laundry, or make all manner of excuses not to take action. All the postponement leaves us tired, fussy, and right where we started.

I have had the best luck in my career when I found something that turned me on, and I went for it, right then and there. Granted, not everything I started turned out well. As a matter of fact, most of the projects I started never saw the light of day. But I learned from every one of those projects, ideas, and concepts. I live my life full of energy, and I focus that energy on moving forward.

Don't waste time, brain cells, or energy asking yourself, "Will this work? What will people think? What if I look or feel stupid? Is this too hard?" Those thoughts are superfluous nonsense. Just start.

For the record, most of what I started I did not finish, but every successful venture in my life was, at one point, just the seed of an idea. If I had not started developing the idea, with energy and massive action, success would have never happened—this book included!

One last thing before we move on: For all of you perfectionists out there, sometimes good enough is good enough. I have the tendency to not want to move forward on projects unless the details seem perfect. Common misconceptions include the feeling that you can't start a company until you know every little detail, can't hire an employee until you have a full onboarding process and employee manual. People worry they can't get married or have a baby until they become financially secure, or the stars line up and their horoscope says it's time. Yes, some things need planning and we can't completely throw caution to the wind, but often, us perfectionists slide down that slippery slope to procrastination. The best way to learn is to screw up and then do it a little bit better. Repeat: there is no trial and error without trial, and there is no learning without doing. In other words, for all you readers who like it as simple as I do, "You can't steer a parked car."

Picture every new venture as venture 1.0 and realize that you can never get to "venture finished product" without version 1.0. Give yourself permission to fail. It's okay to screw up.

KEY CONCEPT

IT'S NOT A FAILURE UNTIL YOU QUIT. ONLY WHEN YOU GIVE UP HAVE YOU TRULY FAILED.

Now that you have your noggin wrapped around that little jewel, get ready for the secret sauce. You might want to sit down for this one:

PERSEVERANCE

Don't have a fancy high-school education as I do? Let me bring it down a notch: *Don't give up, even when the sensible people do.* Check out some quotes from letters written to authors who chose to persevere:

> "Too different from other juveniles on the market to warrant its selling."
>
> —Rejection letter to Dr. Seuss

> "Anthologies don't sell."
>
> —Rejection letter to Jack Canfield and Mark Hansen, authors of ***Chicken Soup for the Soul*** (over 125 million sold)

> "It is so badly written."
>
> —Rejection letter to Dan Brown, author of ***The Da Vinci Code***

> "We feel we don't know the main character well enough."
>
> —Rejection letter to J. D. Salinger, author of ***Catcher in the Rye***

"The girl doesn't, it seems to me, have a special perception or feeling which would lift that book above the 'curiosity' level."

—One of 16 rejection letters written in response to ***The Diary of Anne Frank***

"It was rejected 60 times. But letter number 61 was the one that accepted me. Three weeks later, we sold the book to Amy Einhorn Books."

—Kathryn Stockett, regarding her worldwide best-seller ***The Help***, which was made into a movie.

"An endless nightmare. I think the verdict would be 'Oh don't read that horrid book.'"

—Rejection letter to H. G. Wells, author of ***The War of the Worlds***

"An absurd story as romance, melodrama, or record of New York high life."

—Rejection letter to F. Scott Fitzgerald, author of ***The Great Gatsby***

"It's the worst book I have ever read. I will never get those hours of my life back. I hate the author personally, as a human being, although we have never met. Worst decision of my life."

—DISGRUNTLED READER OF ***I Am a Freaking Genius: Why Don't I have More Money?***

The main difference between successful business owners and failed business owners has to do with giving up. It's not about skill, or education, or background, or privilege, or advantage. Simply getting after it and staying after it until it is done—that's what winners do.

Let's go back to my very first business. If you read the introduction to this book, you may recall I got the entrepreneurial bug early in life, at age 22. I used every penny I had saved to purchase a Service Master franchise. Service Master was an office cleaning service: we took out the trash, cleaned the carpets and floors, and so on. I know it all sounds very glamorous, but it really was hard work.

To qualify, new franchisees were required to fly to Memphis for two weeks and learn how to be business owners/trash-taker-outers. The first week consisted of all of us in a classroom, wearing button-up shirts and ties, with a teacher going over the basics of how to run a business.

I furiously took notes, trying to capture every drop of wisdom the teacher shared. I had no knowledge, no experience, no back-up plan, no savings, and no other options. The veteran business owners and franchisees napped or doodled. During the following week we found ourselves—minus the ties and slacks—

knee deep in waxing products, floor stripper, and dirty toilets. It was a thrill ride.

Two weeks later, I arrived home full of energy and ready to take on the world, as the greatest Service Master franchisee western Colorado had ever seen! The guy I bought the company from only had four to five employees, all of whom were cleaners, and he and his wife ran the business out of their home. I planned on running it out of my apartment. I woke up early to get the newspaper—I am an old man and back in the day, we got an actual paper with news written on it—and as I opened the door, I noticed a lone yellow sticky note hanging precariously on it, flapping ever so gently in the wind. Written boldly and clearly in bright blue ink across it were exactly four words, "'We quit,' the employees."

One helluva good morning!

This would have been a great opportunity to tell myself and my wife we had given it our best and done all we could do, but it hadn't worked out, and we should start looking for another job. That was not an option for me. Everything I had was at stake. I had bet everything on the success of this business. I did the only thing I knew how to do and started interviewing people twice my age at a local restaurant, Pufferbelly's, in Grand Junction, Colorado, during the day to do the cleaning jobs my wife and I were doing at night. I have always had a baby face and looked about 15 years old at the time. From 5 p.m. to 5 a.m. my wife and I cleaned every single office building, school, restaurant, and outhouse on our customer list.

It took months to dig out of the hole, figure out what the heck we were doing, or even get a decent night's sleep. We refused to give up, and less than three years later, we sold the company for more than three times what we paid for it. That money became the seed money for the future investments that have allowed me to sit here in my boxer shorts, happily unemployed, and pontificating on the meaning of life and business for you fine people.

That is a lovely story of perseverance at the macro level, but what most people miss out on is perseverance at the micro level. In order to successfully do anything, one must take care of a dozen little things on a daily basis. So let's talk about what it looks like on a day-to-day basis.

MAKE IT HAPPEN

The minimum-wage employee asks himself, "What is the least I can do and still say that I have been working on it?" while the successful business owner, asks, "What else can I do to move forward right now?"

It can be the difference between taking at his word a vendor who says he will do X right now and following up with him to make sure it actually happens.

Or the difference between calling someone to discuss whatever problem you have right now as opposed to e-mailing that person and using the time you wait for a reply as an excuse to delay doing anything.

There is a difference between "I guess we can't do X because of this obstacle" and "In light of this obstacle, what do I have to change to get X done?"

What would all of this look like for something simple, such as having to buy a building to get your business started?

- You can't lease the building you want? Buy it.
- You don't have the money? Go to the bank.
- That bank tells you your request is insane? Go to every bank within 100 miles.
- Every last one of them tells you to pound sand? Ask your family.
- Your family is broke and/or hates you? Get a hard money loan.
- You can't afford hard money loan interest rates? Take on a partner in the building.
- You can't find a partner? Find someone to buy the building and lease it to you.
- You can't find that person? Beg and plead the owner of the building to finance it.
- The owner refuses? Find a rock-star coach for another idea.
- No one will take your call? Tie yourself to the building and refuse to leave until you get what you want.

I could go on and on, but the idea is that you have not failed until you give up. Never accept the idea that "It's not going to happen." Instead, ask yourself, "What else do I need to do to make this happen?"

A young reporter interviewed Thomas Edison about his electric light bulb experiments. The reporter asked Edison if he felt like a failure and thought he should give up. Perplexed, Edison replied, "Young man, why would I feel like a failure? And why would I ever give up? I now know definitively over 9,000 ways that an electric light bulb will not work. Success is almost in my grasp." Shortly after that, with over 10,000 attempts, Edison invented the light bulb.

This concept works with everything from getting a vendor to deliver as agreed to higher-level actions including the production of every freaking light bulb ever made, thank you very much, Mr. Edison! There is no getting around perseverance.

Watch people who always seem to get things done; their behavior patterns are unmistakable. The doers, owners, and people living the lives that takers and complainers all want, are out there, never giving up, never giving in to the remotest possibility that they may not succeed. They do not ask the world what they can have, or if it would be okay for them to have it. They bend the world to their will and make it what they want.

Think about people who have changed world history, as well as people who seem to be massive producers in your world. Before we move on to the next amazing concept, let me hit you with a fun story that rocked my world when I first read it.

Young Soichiro was born in Japan in 1906 and grew up apprenticing under his father as a blacksmith while his mother worked as a weaver. At age 15, he left home and headed to Tokyo to find work. He became an auto mechanic and returned home at age 22 to start his own shop. He sold everything he owned to develop his concept of a piston ring. He dreamed of selling his idea to Toyota and even hawked his wife's jewelry to keep the business afloat.

When he finally finished what was his life's work, Toyota was not interested. He went to school only to be mocked by professors and students alike who found his designs ridiculous.

After two years of believing and persevering, Toyota actually gave Soichiro a contract for his rings. This was about the time Japan was gearing up for war. The government refused to give Soichiro the necessary concrete to build his factory, a perfect opportunity for Soichiro to throw up his hands, give up, and let life happen. Soichiro refused to give up. He and his team invented a new process for creating their own concrete and built their own factory, which was promptly bombed. Twice.

Time for resignation? Not by a long shot. They collected all the discarded gasoline cans left by American troops, deeming them "gifts from Mr. Truman." They used them as raw materials, which were not available in Japan. Imagine getting bombed and finding a way to create value in your life from such an event.

Soichiro's factory was then decimated by an earthquake.

Finally, unable to continue, he sold what remained of his business to Toyota. Japan had an extreme gas shortage at the time, and Soichiro could not afford gasoline to drive to the store for groceries for his family. Being a man of perseverance, he found a small motor from a lawnmower and attached it to his bicycle, again making the best use of his limited resources. He rode his bike everywhere. Friends, family, and neighbors all wanted one, and he sold every engine and bicycle he could get his hands on but had no resources or capital to continue. Not a man used to giving up, he handwrote 18,000 letters—this was obviously well before the time of Google, laser printers, and e-mail—to bike-shop owners, asking them to invest in his concept. Three thousand of them gave him money, which he used to build his first shipment. It failed, because the machines were too bulky and few people bought them. Still persevering, he stripped the bike down to its bare bones and named it the Super CUB. It was an "overnight" success and went on to win him the Emperor's Award. The man's full name was Soichiro Honda. He went on to start a car company a few of you may be familiar with.

Chapter 2

IT WILL BE UNCOMFORTABLE GETTING RICH, BUT IT'S DOWNRIGHT PAINFUL BEING POOR!

"I just taught my kids about taxes by eating 38 percent of their ice cream."

—Conan O'Brien

"A successful man is one who makes more money than his wife can spend. A successful woman is one who can find such a man."

—Lana Turner

Would it be offensive if I took a minute to say what a great chapter title chapter 2 has? Would that be in bad taste? What the heck, you only live once. It's my book, and that title rocks! People have all sorts of misconceptions about what you have to do to be wealthy or build a multimillion-dollar business. It requires doing what most people won't do, but the flip side is millions of people work themselves to the bone through long and arduous years solely to avoid doing the unpleasant, uncomfortable things they need to do to become wealthy. Insanity!

As a young man in my twenties, I had more success than most of the people in my circle of friends. I invariably got the, "Hey Mike, I notice you are doing pretty well for yourself. Can I take you out to lunch and pick your brain?" Being the helpful, egotistical guy that I am, I always agreed. Oddly enough, very few actually scheduled the lunch.

One quick tangent—that's a lie, there will be many tangents, and they will be long—the few people who did make the lunch happen rarely paid. To this day, I pay for nearly every dinner or lunch I go to with someone less successful than I am. Not a big deal, but it provides an interesting insight into their psyches. These people have the he-has-tons-of-money-and-I-don't syndrome, as opposed to a more effective mindset: "I need this guy's help much more than he needs to help me. The least I can do is offer to buy his lunch. Maybe he will help me in the future."

While not earthshaking, this kind of faulty thinking manifests itself day after day with every person these people meet, in every situation they encounter. It has a large, cumulative, and negative impact. I can't think of a single one of these people who have gone on to great things.

Very few of the people I know who could benefit from help with business or money ever ask for help. Of the few who ask, even fewer follow through with lunch. Almost none of the guys who offer to buy lunch actually buy lunch. The worst part of it all is that of the few who did come to lunch, I can't think of a single one who did what I recommended, followed up with a thank-you, requested another lunch, asked for more information, or had any resulting success.

Looking back, it's clear they wanted easy, comfortable answers. Most of the time they had preconceived notions of what they wanted to hear, and when my advice didn't line up with what they wanted, they did their own thing and, not surprisingly, got the same results as always.

When I started selling cars at age 19, I had conversations with my friends making minimum wage, which was $4.25 per hour at the time or just under $9,000 per year. When I explained to them I worked on commission and only got paid if and when I sold a car, they often said they could never do that, because it was too risky. I made $30K my first year, $40K my second year, and finished my third and final year making $50K. They couldn't work without a guarantee, whereas I couldn't trade an hour of my time for $4 minus taxes. It is important that you define the word risk properly.

This is a key reason for my becoming a business owner. I quickly learned that the person who takes on the risk of making something happen is compensated far better than the people in his or her employ. But it's not only that. There is great risk in working for other people, as your future is dependent on how well they run their business.

Often, the advice I gave people involved taking an easier path than the path they wanted to take. But it would have taken them out of their comfort zone, so they quit before they got started. Let me throw some examples your way:

NUGGET OF WISDOM

Join a mastermind group.

Poor-guy mindset: "Sounds expensive, and they might want to meet at night; I need to relax after a hard day's work."

Soon-to-be rich-guy mindset: "I really don't want to give up a Thursday night, but I can't stomach the thought of working the same job for the next 40 years. Thursday nights it is. Maybe it will even be fun!"

NUGGET OF WISDOM

If you want to start your own business, offer your services for free to get some experience and some great referrals.

Poor-guy mindset: "Work for free? I think not, good sir. I get paid little enough as it is!"

Soon-to-be-rich-guy mindset: "That is super exciting. I had no idea how I was going to get my first gig. Now I can think of a dozen people who would let me do something for free!"

NUGGET OF WISDOM:

Before you go on a job interview, research the company, find out its greatest "pain," learn everything you can about its competitors, and put together a list of questions. Figure out the best way you can help the company achieve its goals. Don't talk about how great you are; talk about what the company needs and how you can help it.

Poor-guy mindset: "That sounds like a ton of work, plus it probably won't work anyway."

Soon-to-be-rich-guy mindset: "Solid idea! With that kind of preparation, maybe I'll apply for a better position to start!"

NUGGET OF WISDOM

I have a great book/seminar that has helped me a ton and answered the questions you are asking me right now better than I can. You should check it out!

Poor-guy mindset: "A book? I read my last book in my senior year of high school, and I am not going to break my streak now! How much does that seminar cost? Are you kidding? I could buy another flat screen TV for that!"

Soon-to-be-rich-guy mindset: "I already read that book, but maybe it's time to revisit it. As far as the seminar is concerned, I am going to get there early and ask the speaker a bunch of questions. I bet there are going to be some other people like me there I can partner with and really get this thing rocking!

NUGGET OF WISDOM

Research how much you spend to acquire a customer and determine what the lifetime value of a customer is and come up with new ways to acquire a customer for less.

Poor-guy mindset: "How am I gonna get all that data? I would need to upgrade my CRM (contact manager), which I am not gonna pay for, and that sounds like a lot of work, and I already know what my customers want."

Soon-to-be-rich-guy mindset: "Great idea. If I really got to know my customers, I could break them up into categories and spend more on the most valuable ones, allowing me to ditch the pain-in-the-butt ones."

Did you notice a pattern? Did you also notice that nothing I asked them to do was as hard as continuing to live the life they are already living? But my suggestions were far enough out of their comfort zone to keep them frozen. I actually have a buddy who is a great guy and wanted to start a business similar to mine. I turned him on to a great resource online, a package of free stuff. He just had to pay the $20 shipping charge, but he couldn't bring himself to do it. Twenty bucks!

Funny thing was we went out to lunch, and I forgot my wallet. He paid the bill and told me not to worry about it. When I recommended the resource to him, we had arrived back at my house, where I handed him the $20 he had already written off in his mind. He was out no money. He sat for ten minutes, stuck in indecision. He finally ordered the materials, but it blew me away to see how small some people's comfort zones are. It made me doubt his willingness to do the difficult work required to build a business.

> "A person's success in life can usually be measured by the number of uncomfortable conversations he or she is willing to have."
>
> —Timothy Ferriss,
> ***The 4-Hour Workweek***

Unsuccessful people see successful people and think, "If only I had his opportunities, I could totally do that." They don't consider that. To get to that point, those successful people spent decades doing things that other people won't do. I was born poor. My mom never owned a car (still doesn't), so if I wanted to get somewhere, my options were walking, bicycle, city bus, and hope. I was raised not knowing any rich people and had no idea we were poor. We always had food, clothes, and shelter. I assumed all those '80s movies of rich people wearing monocles and hanging out at their exclusive clubs nailed it, and I could never be a part of that world. The way I saw it, the rich were born into a fraternity, and I was not. Case closed.

This attitude changed when I was 19 years of age and got a job in which I was exposed to the "real world." I started to discover there is a cause and effect relationship between actions, income, and getting what you want out of life. The only problem was I had zero role models. However, I did have a love of reading and quickly discovered personal development books and, later, business development books. I built a solid foundation of knowledge, but I still had no one to talk to, ask questions of, and figure things out with.

Then, I found my first mastermind group. I thought I had hit the jackpot! All these other like-minded people were not only willing to help me, personally, but also share their experiences, failures, and successes. I finally peeked behind the curtain at the people living the life I wanted. The most exciting thing was they weren't all from "advantaged" situations. They weren't all super geniuses that I couldn't keep up with intellectually. Some were smarter than I was, some not as smart. The things that made these people successful weren't things outside their control. Their success was based on choices, choices they made and choices I could make! Get out your highlighters and notepads because here come the keys to the kingdom.

They didn't give up. They were willing to do whatever it took. They were willing to do uncomfortable things that other people wouldn't do. As simple as it sounds, they believed they could do it. Every successful man, woman, and child I have ever met knew they could do it, 100 percent.

> "Whether you think you can, or you
> think you can't, you're right."
>
> —Henry Ford

Now, for the answers you have all been breathlessly waiting for: How do you put all this newfound knowledge into practice and use it to transform your business into an obedient, moneymaking workhorse? Here are some day-to-day examples of things that aren't all that hard to do and that the vast majority of people just won't do, along with some intriguing statistics.

EVERYONE FAILS BEFORE SUCCEEDING

Seven-figure business owners fail, colossally and in public. They are willing to look stupid. Do they like failing any more than unsuccessful people do? Nope. But they are willing to do it. If that's what it takes, that's what they do. Sometimes you gotta man up. Tim Corley of success.com found that

1. The average millionaire goes bankrupt at least 3.5 times in his life.
2. Seven-figure business owners don't watch a lot of TV and even less reality TV.
    - Sixty-seven percent of wealthy people watch one hour or less of TV every day, versus 23 percent of the poor.
    - Six percent of the wealthy watch reality TV, versus 78 percent of the poor.
3. Seven-figure business owners constantly learn and invest in themselves (kind of like you, buying and actually reading this book!)
    - Sixty-three percent of the wealthy listen to audio books during their commute to work, versus 5 percent of the poor.

- Eighty-eight percent of the wealthy read for 30 minutes or more each day for education or career reasons, versus 2 percent of the poor.
- Eighty-six percent of the wealthy believe in lifelong educational self-improvement, versus 5 percent of the poor.
- Eighty-six percent of the wealthy love to read, versus 26 percent of the poor.

Seven-figure business owners take responsibility for everything, including their own thinking. They don't allow comfortable self-defeating attitudes such as "Why try? It's not going to work out," or "I get all the bad luck." The creed of the poor is "Not my fault and definitely not my responsibility."

When things go wrong, seven-figure business owners are first in line to figure out why and how to change what they did or did not do to get the result they want next time. Others look to place blame, whereas high earners solve problems. **If everything that doesn't work out isn't your fault, you can't make things work out next time. If everything that goes wrong is your fault, you have the power to fix things next time.** This is an example of powerful thinking, as is the following:

- Eighty-four percent of the wealthy believe good habits create opportunity, versus 4 percent of the poor.
- Seventy-six percent of the wealthy believe bad habits create detrimental situations, versus 9 percent of the poor.

Here are a few more fun and insightful tidbits about the wealthy to try on for size:

- A 2010 study argues that millionaires (those in the top 1 percent of earners) pay approximately 40 percent of all taxes in the United States. The media labels this as "not paying their fair share."
- According to the book *The Millionaire Next Door*, only 20 percent of millionaires inherited their wealth. The other 80 percent earned their cash on their own. I guess they weren't "born with it."
- Half of all millionaires are self-employed or own a business. This bodes well for you, a small business owner.
- Most (about 80 percent) modern American millionaires today are first-generation millionaires.
- Twenty-three percent of the wealthy gamble. Fifty-two percent of poor people gamble. A little common sense for ya!
- Eighty-one percent of the wealthy maintain a to-do list of important tasks of the day (doing things most people won't do), versus 19 percent of the poor.
- Sixty-seven percent of the wealthy write down their goals, versus 17 percent of the poor.
- Six percent of the wealthy say what's on their mind, versus 69 percent of the poor. (I found this particularly interesting.)

- Seventy-nine percent of the wealthy network five hours or more each month, versus 16 percent of the poor. This is a great example of doing what is uncomfortable.
- Forty-four percent of the wealthy wake up three hours before work starts, versus 3 percent of the poor.

Are you seeing the pattern of doing what others are unwilling to do?

Chapter 3

THE BUSINESS KILLER YOU NEVER SEE COMING

"You have to stay in shape. My grandmother started walking five miles a day when she was 60. She's 97 today and we don't know where the hell she is."

—Ellen DeGeneres

"If I knew I was going to live this long, I'd have taken better care of myself."

—Mickey Mantle

"I know a man who gave up smoking, drinking, sex, and rich food. He was healthy right up to the day he killed himself."

—Johnny Carson

Welcome to what might be the least popular chapter in this book. Until now, we have spent our time getting to know each other and talking about the habits and mindsets of building a multimillion-dollar business. We have had some laughs, and you are 146 percent more intelligent, but if we don't cover what needs to be covered in this chapter, it could all be for naught.

I am talking about your need to balance your business life with your personal life. I have seen more businesses derailed by lack of balance than just about any issue other than partners. Nearly every partnership I have seen fails, but we are not covering partners in this book. (That was a freebee.) Luckily, there are only two main killers to worry about:

1. Physical health
2. Lack of balance

I am guessing you are already tempted to shut down, turn off, and stop reading, with thoughts such as:

- "I've heard all this before."
- "I already know what I need to do."
- "I tried that, and it didn't work out."
- "I am perfectly balanced and feel great. Stop being so invasive, Mike!"

Just hang with me for just a couple of pages. This is not your doctor towing the "doctor company line," someone selling a weight loss program, or your spouse telling you what to do. This is a fellow, in-the-trenches entrepreneur, who has walked in your shoes, and we are talking business owner to business owner. Read the chapter. Give it a fair hearing in your mind, and if you still aren't picking up what I am laying down, throw the book into the nearest fire, shake your fist at the heavens, and commence with the angry e-mails.

Fear not. At no point in this chapter are we going to hold hands, form a drum circle, or sing "Kumbaya" around a campfire. We are going to talk about practical things that blindside business owners, often after it's too late to correct the problems they cause.

It always amazes me how business owners pour everything they have into their business but completely ignore their health and relationships until one of them goes horribly wrong and hits them over the head with a two-by-four. I have been guilty of this too, fellas. When a health or relationship disaster happens, instantly and magically, priorities change. The business that you sacrificed everything for seems worthless compared to the personal crisis staring you in the face.

At that time in the game—for me, this was during my divorce—the available options are limited and generally unpleasant. The good news is if you are willing to make some adjustments to a few key habits now, you will enjoy massive benefits for the rest of your life. If you ignore these key habits, the payments and interest on these areas of your life come due, but when you don't make the payments, they accrue, and a nasty balloon payment shows up that you will probably be unable to make.

Let's start with number one: your body. We all get exactly one, and it's the only place we have to live. There are two ways you can move the meter on this one:

1. When you put crap in your body

2. When you don't exercise (I tried to think of a more fun way to put that but couldn't come up with it. I owe you one.)

Let's jump on the putting-crap-in train.

ALCOHOL

I will be upfront with you on this one. I never really drank, so this may be one of the few areas where I have not walked in your shoes. I have an A-type, addictive, take-it-to-the-extreme personality. For me, not drinking is probably a good thing. Every time I tell people I don't drink, they ask me one of three questions. I'll go ahead and answer those for you in advance.

1. Yes, really… I don't drink…

2. No, I've never had a "problem" with alcohol.

3. No, I am not Mormon.

Disclaimer: I have no moral, spiritual, or emotional angst surrounding alcohol. My wife and most of my favorite people drink socially, so everything that follows is based solely on what I have observed, not because of a religious or anti-alcohol bias.

I have observed four ways in which people use alcohol:

- Complete abstinence
- Moderate drinking
- Occasional, or not so occasional, binge drinking

- Full-blown addiction

Let's take a gander at each one.

COMPLETE TEETOTALER

The pros and cons are:

> **Pros:** Little risk of becoming addicted. You don't have to worry about morning-after regrets. Not drinking eliminates a source of empty carbs and sugars. No hangovers. No sadness when drinking isn't an option. No feeling that you need a drink to get through a certain event. Teetotalers never worry about drinking and driving, the potential jail time, or killing or maiming themselves and others in an accident.
>
> **Cons:** Missing out on "being part of the group" when out with friends. Having to "babysit" when others are drunk is no fun. When you don't drink, you do not have the ability to enjoy drinking. Some people feel uncomfortable around nondrinkers. I have heard, many a time, "I don't trust anyone who doesn't drink" from people who didn't know I didn't drink—and from a few who did!

Although I recognize this is probably not the category most of you fall into, I just wanted to point out that it can be done. When I explain to people that I don't drink, most of them shake their head and say, "I could never do that." I call BS on that. Choosing to drink is fine, but don't fool yourself into believing you could never stop doing it. It is possible and, quite frankly, not even that hard. So drink, or don't drink, but either way, make the decision and own it!

MODERATE DRINKER

The pros and cons are:

Pros: These people get to enjoy going out more. For them, alcohol is a nice way to relax and a good social lubricant. Life is good, and they carry none of the social stigma of teetotalers. Some studies show health benefits associated with moderated drinking.

Cons: There's a risk of drinking too much, drinking and driving, and becoming addicted. Also, alcohol is a lot of empty carbs and sugar.

BINGE DRINKER/ADDICT

We don't have to go into binge drinking, alcohol addiction, or drug use. I can't come up with a single pro, and the cons are well documented. They are also outside the scope of this book. If you choose either of these routes, it is going to be hard to build and sustain a seven-figure business. It will be even harder to sustain any quality of life. I'm not trying to get preachy. I just call 'em as I see 'em. A little common sense goes a long way here.

If I lost you, as a friend, at the beginning of this chapter, you might just downright hate this next one: refined sugar.

REFINED SUGAR

Unlike our friend alcohol, I have first-hand experience with this bad boy and have been addicted to it for most of my life. I included it because it is subtly addictive and influences mood, energy, sleep, and the ability to focus at work. These factors affect a person's ability to grow and manage a business and the stress that goes along with it. Refined sugar wreaks havoc in your body, creating an energy spike-crash merry-go-round that flat out sucks. Very few people are even aware they are addicted to it or what an amazing life awaits at the other side of that addiction.

Earlier this year, I quit, cold turkey, refined sugar and caffeine, though I still eat fruit. I thought it was going to be rough, so I planned three to four days of not needing to get much done and having the ability to sleep a lot if I wanted to. I did have some headaches, which I believe were from caffeine withdrawal. I felt sleepy, a little grumpy, and foggy headed, but after being sugar- and caffeine-free for four days, I got an insane amount of energy and felt great. I was energized and felt amazing. That lasted about three weeks before I transitioned into a now-normal high-energy lifestyle. In addition to losing weight, I feel great. Prior to this transition, I tried to "eat clean" and lose weight, but I always returned to eating crap. This time, cutting sugar, caffeine, and fast food seemed much more sustainable. They are addictive, and once I got through the withdrawal stage, I had no more cravings. I still want to put junk in my body now and again, but it is more habit than addiction and very manageable.

When I was living the sugar-high, "crash" lifestyle, I didn't notice how much I depended on sugar or caffeine and how lethargic I felt when not on my high. I felt I needed those things to be creative, or to focus on work, or do anything that wasn't sitting on my butt and watching TV. I know this dietary advice sounds extreme, but I couldn't help including it, since eliminating sugar and caffeine has had such a positive impact on my life and was much easier than I thought it would be. Your results may vary, but I have had too good an experience not to share it, and my ability to focus on work has grown. Even if you don't quit cold turkey, limiting sugar intake can change your life for the better!

EXERCISE

The second piece of advice for keeping the ol' body in tip-top shape concerns exercise—with weights. I adopted this habit about ten years ago. When I started, I hadn't worked out in well over a decade since graduating from high school. I had "wanted" to go to the gym for years and finally got fed up with that flabby jerk in the mirror and took action. I wasn't a mess at six feet tall and weighing about 200 pounds, but I was certainly not in shape.

The tipping point for me was hiring a top-notch personal trainer. The guy I hired charged $1,500 per month, for three sessions per week, and he was worth every penny of it. We didn't just workout together; he interviewed me about my goals, weighed me, took before, during, and after body-fat measurements, and pictures. He had me record everything I ate, measured biceps, chest, waist, shoulders, thighs, and calves. While we worked out, he constantly educated me on nutrition, the benefits of lean muscle, how to build lean muscle, overall health, and how to achieve my personal goals. Although I could afford it, I was too cheap to pay a guy and then not show up. So, I showed up. I have hired the services of cheaper, fresh-out-of-training-school alternatives, who just tell you what exercises to do. For me, they didn't stick. I am not saying you have to spend $1,500/ month on a trainer, I am saying that you need a high level of commitment that is willing to invest in your health.

During the first two weeks, I hated everything about the exercise program. I didn't want to go. I didn't want to be there when I was there, and I felt sore when I wasn't there. Weeks three through eight, I actually started to look forward to going to the gym but still did not enjoy being there or working out. I didn't mind the soreness anymore; it made me feel I was building muscle. After two months of dragging myself to the gym, the hook was set. I looked forward to going, enjoyed working out, and felt great overall. It took me two unhappy months to create a habit that has served me well for the last decade. My net worth is much higher due to working out. I have more energy on workout days and get more done.

For me, it was easier to maintain the exercise routine with a workout partner. I seem to have no problem letting myself down by staying in my warm bed at 6 a.m., but if I know I'm committed to working out with someone who is waiting for me at the gym, I haul my lazy butt out of bed and go! Once you get addicted, you will want to work out even when traveling or on vacation. It produces a natural high when you are engaged in activities that don't involve a lot of lounging around.

Over the years, I've spent tens of thousands of dollars on trainers and nutritional guidance. Aerobics and weight training are different. One is not better than the other; they simply serve different purposes.

Aerobic exercise is best for burning fat. You want to keep your heart rate elevated and level, not rising and falling. You should be able to talk but not easily. For me, this is around 150 bpm. If you reach a heart rate at which you are unable to talk without gasping for breath, you are in anaerobic territory which runs the risk of burning muscle, not fat. Aerobic exercise is good for your heart and for burning fat. If you eat well, you shouldn't need a lot of this. When you perform aerobic exercise, you burn calories while exercising. When you stop exercising, you stop burning calories.

There is no such thing as "toning." You either build lean muscle, or you don't. You either lose the fat around the muscle, or you don't. Those are your only two options.

Weight training is not ideal for calorie burning, although it is a nice bonus. The goal of weight lifting is to build lean muscle. This has all manner of benefits. In men, it increases testosterone, naturally, which can improve your sex drive, sleep, and overall energy. Lean muscle uses 15 percent more energy to maintain than fat and burns calories 24 hours a day, even while you sleep. As we age, our bodies naturally wear out, with loss of muscle and bone density. Adding lean muscle to your body helps you live longer, increases bone density, and improves quality of life during your later years. Take note of the older people you see. Often, they are stooped over and not very mobile. If you build the habit of keeping lean muscle, this will not be your future.

Your heart rate spikes when you lift weights and drops when you stop swinging between the anaerobic and resting ranges. Lifting weights tears your muscles, which then rebuild themselves more strongly. This is why it is important to rest your muscles and not work out with weights every day. When lifting weights, you burn calories, and when your workout ends, your body continues in a calorie-burning overdrive for the next 48 hours. If you work out every two days, you will be in a constant state of heightened calorie burning. Personally, I have found three times per week is best. Less than that is not a habit, and I get limited results. When I work out more than that, I don't look forward to going to the gym as much and I tend to get burned out.

Let's do some time math. My workouts are fairly intense and usually last about 45 minutes. If you figure it takes 30 minutes to get ready and go to the gym and back, when you add the 45 minutes at the gym, the total is one hour and 15 minutes of commitment per workout. This makes a grand total of three hours and 45 minutes each week. There are 112 waking hours in each week, assuming you sleep eight hours every night. Three hours and 45 minutes is less than 4 percent of your waking hours. As far as concerns the return on investment (ROI), you will not find one much better than that.

Don't make the mistake many inexperienced trainers make of trying to combine weight lifting and cardio. You will likely get the worst of both worlds. Because you are lifting weights, you will be swinging between anaerobic, muscle eating mode and resting. Neither of those are ideal for burning fat. If you lift small weights with many reps, you are probably not building any lean muscle. Big weights = big muscles. Little weights = little muscles.

There is no such thing as "toning." You either build lean muscle, or you don't. You either lose the fat around the muscle, or you don't. Those are your only two options. Build or lose muscle, and build or lose fat. Your body and your genes dictate what shape those muscles grow into, and where the fat dissolves first. Not good for selling diet plans, but it is the truth.

Adopting these habits teaches discipline. If you are unable to discipline yourself to exercise, it is unlikely you will be able to discipline yourself in other ways. The man who wakes up in pitch-black darkness at 5:30 a.m. and leaves his warm, comfortable bed for the gym is the man who is going to have the testicular fortitude to do the things it will take to grow his business.

Let's sum up the three things you can do to get the most benefit, the "low-hanging fruit":

- Limit or eliminate alcohol and drugs.
- Don't eat addictive sugar and caffeine.
- Work out with weights three times per week.

That might sound like a lot, but those are all habits created like any other habit. Once you develop them, they become easy to maintain, and your entire life will benefit from them.

UNBALANCED RELATIONSHIPS

The next business killer is an unhealthy, singular focus on your business. This can create a failure to develop healthy relationships, hobbies, and reasons to live that go beyond your business. I did not have this down during most of my twenties and still struggle with it, periodically. To be clear, there are times for business owners—

such as when I bought my first business and all the employees quit—when they must go all out and be a little insanely focused on accomplishing something, but when that turns into a lifestyle, as opposed to weeks or months of hyper-focused activity, you are likely heading for trouble.

My wife did not appreciate the insanity and divorced me. Suddenly, the business I sacrificed everything to grow was not even on my radar. I realized all that desire to be successful was only important in my family context. I wanted to make the money to do nice things with them, spend time with wife and son, but when the business overtook my family life, I lost it all. Two of the top five reasons for bankruptcy are health issues and divorce.

The six areas of your life that must be in balance for your seven-figure business to be a blessing and not a curse are physical health, family, and your spiritual, financial, intellectual, and social life.

If you follow the concepts in this book, financial gains will be no problem. If you follow the concepts in this chapter, you will feel better and perform at a higher level than 96 percent of the people out there. It is beyond the scope of this book to dive deeply into spiritual, family, intellectual, or social issues, but the key is balance.

What good is having a private jet if you are too obese or in too poor health to fly and enjoy travel and/or have no one to travel with?

What good is the dream house you have always wanted if you are never there or there is nobody to share it with?

The 80-year-old, divorced billionaire who has no relationship with his children and a gnarled dying body would trade everything he owns to have the opportunities you likely have right now. The mortality rate for humans is darn near 100 percent. As we age, our spiritual life becomes more important. Only bad things come from waiting until old age to deal with such issues.

Thanks for sticking with me through this not-entirely business strategy chapter. I hesitated to include it, but it has been so foundational in my life I felt I would cheat you if I were to leave it out. Let's finish up with a couple of statistics that make me sound as if I know what I am talking about. Best-selling author Tom Corley found that

- Seventy percent of the wealthy eat less than 300 junk-food calories per day, whereas 97 percent of the poor eat more than 300 junk-food calories per day.
- Seventy-six percent of the wealthy exercise aerobically four days a week, whereas only 23 percent of the poor do this.

Part Two

LET'S TALK ABOUT YOUR BUSINESS

"We were hoping to build a small, profitable company and, of course, what we've done is build a large, unprofitable company."

—Jeff Bezos, founder and CEO of amazon.com

Chapter 4

WHERE SHOULD WE START? HOW ABOUT AT THE BEGINNING?

"Would you tell me, please, which way I ought to go from here?"

"That depends a good deal on where you want to get to," said the Cat.

"I don't much care where ...," said Alice.

"Then it doesn't matter which way you go," said the Cat.

—Lewis Carroll,
Alice in Wonderland

"When I was five years old, my mother always told me that happiness was the key to life. When I went to school, they asked me what I wanted to be when I grew up.

I wrote down "happy." They told me I didn't understand the assignment, and I told them they didn't understand life."

—ANONYMOUS

Okay, boys and girls, the free ride is over. It's time to get to work! I hope you have been taking notes and marking this book up, but here is where you get to actually do some work. Since the concepts we will cover are general, you will want to write down how you are going to apply them to your business.

VISION, CORE VALUES

There is a lot of noise out there about vision statements. I like simple ideas. People like simple ideas. Let's make this simple. James Collins and Jerry Porras, in their book *Built to Last*, introduce the concept of the big hairy audacious goal (BHAG). The book encourages companies to define visionary goals that are strategic and emotionally compelling. Your BHAG is what you want to accomplish in the next 10–30 years in business. I have adopted the BHAG concept for my companies, and think it is a great way to look at a company vision.

As the name implies, the goal needs to be big, big enough to encourage customers to do business with you and, more importantly, big enough to inspire employees to jump wholeheartedly onto your bandwagon. I like to think of it as my get-me-out-of-bed-in-the-morning rally call. I don't want to get too mired down in this because you, as the owner of your company, must define your BHAG for yourself in a way that ignites your passion. The only rules are that it has to be measurable, exciting, and awe inspiring! Microsoft's BHAG, in the '70s, was to have a desktop computer in every home. At the time, it was so big, hairy, and audacious it was almost laughable, but it got Microsoft's staff out of bed every morning. Only a few decades later, their goal was achieved, and they had to update their BHAG.

Once you have your big, hairy, audacious goal, you have the framework for short-term goals. Once I have my BHAG, I don't make any goals for more than a year out, and I break them down into quarterly focuses or themes. Three months is long enough to get things done alongside running the day-to-day operations of your business but short enough to make noticeable progress weekly, if not daily. Below, you will find some space to write and figure out your BHAG and break it down into what you want to accomplish this year. Then, you will set your quarterly goals.

BHAG *(big hairy audacious goal)*

This year's goal *(should fall in line with your BHAG)*

Quarterly objectives *(your goal for the year, broken into four parts)*

I know all of this sounds like a lot, because it is. This process might take a couple of months to do. Don't get discouraged if there are lots of revisions. I know of no business owners who shut the door to their offices and emerge 12 hours later with a complete and finished BHAG. This is also a process that a good coach can help you to carry out light-years faster.

CORE VALUES

Now that you have a foundation, allow me to get on my soapbox about one of my favorite topics: core values. Once you have your core values, so much of the hassle and stress of hiring, training, and management of your people and business will seem to evaporate, as we will discuss later in the book. You don't decide on your core values so much as you discover them. For years, I asked myself, my family, and those I worked with questions about what I valued most. Since I discovered them, my core values have remained mostly the same for the last 10 years, over multiple businesses. They are personal core values that I live out as part of my business life. This is helpful because it allows and encourages me to be the same person at work as I am at home. That's a lovely place to be in your life.

Another benefit of living by a strong, clear set of core values is that you will automatically attract—and repel—the kind of customer, employee, vendor, and partner you want—or don't want. Your core values will resonate with some people so deeply they will want to work for you, but the people who absolutely don't believe in your core values will never apply.

Disclaimer: none of this happens for merely "having" core values. It only happens when you live, breathe, eat, and sleep your core values.

To make this concept clearer and provide some actionable ideas, I share my core values below:

1. Be real.
2. Have fun.
3. Make money.
4. Help out.

Notice they are all action words. There is a powerful difference between "fun," as a core value, and "have fun," and an equally strong difference between "profit" and "make money." When possible, use action words; they tend to resonate better with people. Let's take a look at how my values have played out in this book:

1. **Be real:** You may have noticed I share the good and the bad and don't try to make myself out as an expert who "never made a mistake." I write this book as if you were sitting across from me and we were working on your business. You are getting the real me, for better or worse!

2. **Have fun:** Hopefully, you have enjoyed reading this book. I've had fun writing it. I know I like a section or sentence when, as I sit here at my computer, typing, I laugh to myself like a psychiatric patient. That, friends, is the core value of having fun.

3. **Make money:** This book and the coaching that I do are for-profit endeavors. As passionate as I am about small business owners and saving them the headaches I went through, this book costs money, and those who coach and mastermind with me pay me. I am not ashamed to charge well for my services, nor should you be.

4. **Help out:** By now, I hope, it is abundantly clear that I love to help business owners. I could do a thousand things for money. I choose to work with people I care about on projects I am passionate about. This flows over to my personal life as well. My wife and I are committed to using the resources God has blessed us with to help causes near and dear to us rather than spending an abundance of time and money making ourselves fat, happy, and comfortable.

Those are examples of how my core values, hopefully, come across in this book. Chances are you own a business and are not writing a book. Read on for examples of how my core values shaped the contracting business I started, grew, and sold.

- **Be real:** This core value is so cool. We put on no pretense. We never acted bigger or more "professional" than we were. We let our individual personalities shine through every aspect of our operation. Customers, vendors, and prospective employees all picked up on it and wanted to be a part of it. This made going to work amazing. Maybe this is why reality shows are so popular, but however you slice it, we, as a team, enjoyed a workplace where we could be ourselves, and the customers loved the vibe as well.

- **Have fun:** This fits in so well with the "be real" part. We had foosball tables in the shop and played every day. Everyone from me down to the entry-level employees participated in foosball tournaments. We invited our customers and their families, and we would be silly. Initially, it was scary and felt risky. We worked with architects, city planners, and general contractors on multimillion-dollar projects. (I tell you this to remove the dreaded excuse of "That's great for you, but it would never work in my business.") I thought they would be too professional for our nonsense. It turned out they needed a break and some fun in their lives, and they loved dealing with real, fun people. They referred everyone they knew.

- **Make money:** None of the things our business provided for customers could be accomplished without money. We charged enough to give killer service without having to nickel and dime our customers, and we still made sure we exceeded expectations. We paid our people more than we had to pay them. Having fun is hard to do if you aren't making any money, as is being real. It was nice to be able to tell our customers we were in business for the money. If they didn't want to, or couldn't, pay, they didn't work with us. Customers found it refreshing.

- **Help out:** This bad boy was the secret sauce for us. On a weekend trip to the barrios of Mexico to build houses for strangers, I built stronger relationships with people I didn't know than I built with people I worked with for years. Helping the community not only brings your team together in a way that nothing else can but is also a ton of fun and brings out the real person in you. Also, the only way we are able to give back revolves around making money.

Now that you are armed with some general examples of how my core values work in this book and worked in one of my businesses, let me give you some specific actionable ideas that I have used in my businesses. Feel free to steal them, and put them into practice in your business today:

- All of my business cards, for years, have had the title of "Janitor."
- All e-mails, business cards, bids, proposals, stationery, web pages, and literature had our core values on them.
- In the About Us section of the website, we put fun pictures and profiles of the employees—what they liked to do and how they helped out in their personal lives.
- At every meeting, employees had the opportunity to share how they lived out a core value that week or how they observed a fellow employee living out the core values.
- We used jobbing.com to find some candidates. They came to do a video for our website, introducing people to our company. They used it to teach the rest of their

team how to make videos for customers. You can have a ton of fun and impart a lot of personality with video.

- We held events for employees, vendors, and customers to serve the community. Sometimes, we would just order food and drinks and invite customers to our shop to play foosball and network. At other times, we would invite small groups of customers to a restaurant for lunch to get their opinions on how to improve, we would always end up with a ton of testimonials and even some referrals. It was a ton of fun and good for business.
- We had a "sexy English automated attendant" direct the calls on our phone system. Instead of getting frustrated when a live person didn't answer their call, customers called back and sometimes had their coworkers call back to listen to her again and again.
- Our "on hold music" was our sexy English automated attendant talking about our core values over music in a fun way—people would actually ask to be put back on hold so they could hear the entire loop.
- Employees could take up to five days a year, with pay, to serve in the community.

I mentioned earlier in this chapter that when you live your core values, much of the work of "management" goes away. Let's get into what this looks like so you can intentionally create it in your organization. We will go over employees and management in more detail in chapter 9, but this foundation centered on your core values is an excellent starting point. For example, instead of asking my employees to read pages and pages of dos and don'ts, I made 90 percent of my management responsibilities consist of asking three questions:

- Did that decision represent our core values?
- Did you feel that decision was right for the customer?
- Did you feel that decision was right for the company?

If the answer to these three questions was yes, nine times out of eight, we knew it was the right decision. Instead of having to come up with the answer to every circumstance any employee might run into, we let the core values do the heavy lifting and be the foundation for answers.

UNIQUE SELLING PROPOSITION (USP)

The last piece of this puzzle is having a solid unique selling proposition (USP). You may have heard of this concept before, and you may even have a USP, but this concept is so foundational I urge you to read through the rest of the chapter just in case you can pick up a nugget of truth you didn't know before. I find that when I work with customers who have a rock-star USP, they are light-years ahead of those who have a weak USP or no USP at all.

Your USP should clearly and simply state the unique benefit your company provides for your customers, not what you like about your company, or why your mom thinks you are special. It has to be **unique to your business and focused on your customers' needs.** Most of your marketing materials—bid presentations, Facebook posts, direct mail pieces, TV and radio spots, elevator pitches, and the like—should be focused on your customer. The only universal thing of interest to your customers is how they will benefit from your product or service. Here are some examples:

- When it absolutely, positively has to be there overnight;
- The milk chocolate melts in your mouth, not in your hand;
- You get fresh, hot pizza delivered to your door in 30 minutes or less, or it's free;
- The night-time, coughing-achy-sniffling-stuffy-head-fever, so-you-can-rest medicine;
- Fifteen minutes could save you 15 percent or more on car insurance.

I intentionally didn't put the names of the companies next to their USPs, but I guess you knew every one of them instantly. Did you notice all of them are customer focused and make it clear why the customer would choose them over the variety of other options available to them, including not doing anything or buying anything? The pizza USP example is so strong it can be credited as foundational to the entire pizza delivery industry.

Now that you are properly fired up and motivated, let's review some Freaking Genius questions to get you started on your USP:

1. What do you naturally do well in your personal life?
2. What does your company uniquely excel at?
3. What are your best customers' unique pains/goals? Why do they buy from you instead of your competitor or instead of doing nothing at all?

4. How can what you and your company do best help solve your top customers' pain and help them achieve their goals? Bonus points if your USP actually identifies your customer.

5. What do your customers want and need that is not being offered? How can you offer it?

6. Another way to ask this is to ask what drives your customers nuts. How can you fix it for them?

7. What is it like to be one of your customers dealing with your company? How is it unique compared to your competitors? How can you make it unique and uniquely better?

8. Is your USP exciting enough to make your customers care?

9. Does your USP sound, or read, like something you and your employees would naturally say?

10. Does your USP spark conversations, questions, and excitement?

Do not confuse table stakes with USPs. Table stakes are things such as friendly service, good quality, and low prices. They are neither unique nor USPs. These phrases are what all competitors say about themselves, and they are the bare minimum standard to be in business. You must offer something unique and customer focused.

Before you decide this is too hard and give up, let me give you the flip side: what happens when you don't offer customers a unique, customer-focused reason to do business with you. In the best-case scenario, your customers still want what you offer and are still aware of you, even though you don't offer them any compelling reason to be. They want your product or service, but the only way they can decide between you and your competitor is price. I'll give away the ending: the lowest price wins, and you start competing based on who can charge the least without going out of business. That's a terrible game. Don't play it. That's your best-case scenario when your USP fails. The worst case is when nobody remembers you at all, and you fade into oblivion. Ouch!

Let's end with the benefits of a clear and compelling vision, paired with a powerful set of core values. When you have these in place, **no one can compete with you.** When I had my contracting business, several businesses tried to "be like us," and it never worked. We were the only ones like us, and the other businesses violated our Be Real core value by trying to imitate us. By trying to be like some other business, they were not "being real." They were faking. It's hard to have fun when you try to be someone or something else. You are the only one who can truly be you. Once you have these pieces in place, your business will be the primary resource for providing the goods or services that consumers want. People with whom your core values resonate will not be happy doing business anywhere else, for any price. This is a game changer, folks. Don't give up on this. Once you pour this solid foundation, every other part of your business gets much easier.

Putting it all together, here is some space to scratch in:

USP (remember it should be unique and customer focused):

Core values (What is ultimately important to you? Make these values action words!):

Chapter 5

SET IT AND FORGET IT

"The factory of the future will have only two employees, a man and a dog. The man will be there to feed the dog. The dog will be there to keep the man from touching the equipment."

—Warren G. Bennis, advisor to Ronald Reagan and John F Kennedy

THE POWER OF EFFICIENCY

Set it and forget it means "do a little work and move on with your life, while your business keeps cranking out cash." What sort of dream-world hokum am I peddling here? None. There is a way to achieve this fairytale utopia. It is all about systems.

There are two kinds of readers out there:

Reader #1 hears the word systems and says to himself, "This is for me. The man writing this is touched by God with genius, and I will have these systems of which he speaks." If this is you, dear reader, you will do just fine. Read the next few sentences along with me and feel free to judge the other half of readers.

> **Reader #2** (boo, hiss) thinks, "I don't need systems. That is probably business-jerk-speak for a lot of work and wasted time."

This next chapter might sting a little, but it can change your life. Buckle up and read on!

You, your life, and everything you have experienced so far is the result of a system. There are ineffective systems, and there are effective systems, systems that create the result that you want and systems that create a different result. Let's illustrate this using something as simple as the gas indicator light coming on in your vehicle:

- Potential system: Ignore the gas light. When the car stops, call your congressman and complain you have been discriminated against, unfairly treated, and your evil, rich neighbors have all the gas in the world. Demand immediate and decisive governmental action!
- Potential system: Ignore the gas light, and when the car stops moving, walk to the nearest car dealer and purchase a new car. (That's my kind of system!)
- Potential system: When the gas light comes on, ignore it for 48.5 miles and then panic while you search frantically for a gas station.
- Potential system: Pay attention to the gas gauge and, as it gets low, consider your plans for the next day and determine the easiest, most efficient time to stop for gas so you aren't trying to fill up when running late for a meeting.

- Potential system: Move to San Francisco, New York, Chicago, or any other metro area that doesn't really require a car. Walk, bike, or take a cab, and never get gas again.

- Potential system: Pay somebody to drive you everywhere and handle the refueling, oil changing, car washing, tire rotating ugliness you dislike.

Do you see how just one tiny action in a day can have a tremendous impact on your day, or even your life? Imagine walking to a car dealer in July, in Phoenix, in 109-degree weather. Picture never filling your tank again because your driver handles those sorts of details. The systems you follow create your life whether you intentionally create them or not.

Efficiency is the natural byproduct of good systems. Inefficiency and frustration are the natural byproducts of bad systems. A pattern I noticed in my life, and in the lives of other highly effective people who get a ton of work done, is efficiency. For example, I don't maintain my lawn or clean my own pool. I pay guys $10–$20 per hour to do it for me, and I don't have to think about it. This frees up energy for activities I am great at, which, coincidentally, pay substantially better than what my pool and yard guys earn. I, generally, enjoy these activities more and they give me energy, as opposed to sucking energy out of me.

I know guys (think Steve Jobs) who wear the same thing every day. They make a single decision about what clothes make them look and feel good, stock up on those clothes, and maybe revisit that issue every five years or so. Shopping is dealt with once. No time is spent picking out clothes on a daily basis. The clothes they choose are comfortable and require no dry-cleaning or pressing. Guys like this are either insane or ingenious or, often, both, but they get a tremendous amount done. The way they approach their wardrobe is an insightful peek into the madness.

As silly as these little decisions are, many of the sheeple out there don't think about any options outside the box. Why have you never thought about the abundant options available to you regarding gas retrieval before today? The answer is that you are not out of your mind, or you already have your own system that works for you. Take this opportunity to think through other more important systems that govern your business and personal life and the results they are creating. **Consider what systems you can intentionally change with the least effort for the most result.** Often, this isn't just a way to be more efficient but a way to increase quality of life merely by spending more of your one, nonrenewable resource (time) on the things you enjoy rather than day-to-day minutia.

Our lives are governed by systems, whether we acknowledge them or not. Most we have developed subconsciously. Some are good; some are bad. The key is to recognize we are constantly using systems, and the quality of our outcomes is directly dependent on the quality of our systems.

Take charge of your systems, and take charge of your life!

Now that we are all on the same, systems-are-great-and-powerful page, let's lay out how these systems show up in your business. Most companies are comfortable with having systems in the product creation or service fulfillment part of their business, and often in their accounting processes, but they often miss the boat when it comes to systematizing the rest of the operation such as hiring and sales and marketing. Let's start with something a little trickier such as interacting with people, so you can see how systems work throughout your business. Without systems, running a small business can be like herding cats. Let's walk through the options:

1. Hire good people who take all of the information available and make excellent decisions (systems in their mind) most of the time. These people are very hard to find, cost a ton of money, and require lots of care and handling.

2. Empower your team to think through the tasks that compose their jobs, write down the most correct way to do those jobs, and change as necessary. This is a one-time task that needs very little care and handling once these systems are implemented.

I am a big fan of number two. Not on board yet? Let me lay out the case against option number one.

If you have been in business for any amount of time, you know that while "hiring great people" is easy to say, it can drive you to drink. These great people are usually already employed, cost a lot of money, and are actively recruited away to other companies. They are also human beings. Human beings get sick, get hit by buses, get pregnant, go on vacation, get divorced, have terrible days, are controlled by emotions, and exhibit all the other characteristics that make humans a pain in the butt. I am not saying it can't work, but business is hard enough without having to find great people. This book is all about reducing brain damage and increasing revenue without increasing your hours worked.

Let's take a look at the land of milk and honey promised by option number two. What are the benefits of creating good systems? A good system works all the time, does not require a weekly paycheck, will not leave for a competitor, never has a bad day, takes maternity leave, goes postal, or demands more benefits, and so on and so forth.

Basically, an average employee equipped with a superior set of systems and procedures can work nearly as effectively as a highly compensated employee with no systems.

Still not jumping for joy? Let the genius continue. One of these days, you might become sick of selling widgets (although I can't imagine why; widgets are awesome!) As a result, you decide to sell your business. Before you jump out of your chair, shake your fist at the heavens and scream, "I will never sell my business," remember you are "selling" your business every day. Every time you hire a new employee, woo a bank or lender, take on a new vendor, try to get a new customer, or keep an old customer, you are selling your business.

Most business sellers get fooled into thinking the customer is buying their lease, their employees (although I don't think it's legal to sell people), their customer list (which actually is a good part of the value), their snazzy logo, some equipment, computers, office furniture, and the like. If and when you do sell your entire business, a well-oiled machine that hums along without depending on you is far, far more valuable than a business dependent on you and on all of your staff staying. A buyer won't pay for that. Every day you don't sell your business, you are buying it. Why not make it as valuable as possible?

The average McDonald's does $2.6 million in sales, with over $150K in profit, and the highest paid employee makes well under $50K per year. Turnover in the fast food business is brutal. Due in large part to a tremendous set of systems and processes, McDonald's has an extremely stable income. Those systems position McDonald's to have a multiyear waiting list of people who will pay the company hundreds of thousands of dollars upfront and a generous percentage of sales for the duration of their franchise.

It is possible for me to walk each and every one of you through this process in your business, but you have to pay me entirely too much money. So let me give you some examples of what this would look like for you on a day-to-day basis. Picture what a well-systematized (read low stress, high profit, and big payday when you sell it) business looks like:

1. **Scenario:** A prospective customer calls in (as a result of one of your many marketing systems). The system dictates how the phone is answered, on what ring, and by whom. It dictates what is said, what happens when the assigned person is not there, on the other line, or unavailable as well as what happens when calls come in after hours.

2. **Scenario:** The prospective customer wants to talk to a salesperson. The system dictates whether this is a customer you want, who gets that call, how the customer's information collected, how the customer's order processed when the customer buys, what happens

when the customer doesn't buy, and what happens when they buy one level of product versus another.

3. **Scenario:** The prospective customer buys something. The system dictates who takes the money and what forms of payment are acceptable—cash, check credit card, or invoice. It spells out how and when the product or service is provided, what quality control measures are in place, how the customer satisfaction is tracked, and how testimonials and referrals are obtained.

Let's take a look at what systems would look like for hiring.

1. **Scenario:** You need to hire a new employee: The system dictates how you determine if you actually need someone and how you determine compensation. Can the job be done by a contractor instead? How do you get applicants? How many applicants are sufficient to make a good hire? What does the interview process look like? How do you make an offer to a prospective employee? What does the "onboarding" process look like when you do hire that person? All questions clearly laid out in the system.

2. **Scenario:** You have the feeling an employee is no longer a good fit: The system dictated the job description at the time of hire, when and how employee reviews were conducted, and what accountability is in place. How do you terminate the employee? Who is in the room? How is the employee escorted from the business? Is there a severance package? Is there an exit interview? In today's insanely litigious universe, these systems are

your best bet to stay out of court and focus on growing your business!

3. **Scenario:** Money needs to come in and go out, and you would prefer it not be stolen: Your system dictates who receives money and answers questions like: Do you take cash? Where do the bank statements go and who opens them? Who can write checks? Who can sign checks? Who can approve bills? Are there redundancies overseeing key transactions? If you are not going to be at your business 24/7 and would like to be able to sleep at night, it is imperative you have strong internal controls around all accounting processes.

I know all this system talk can be overwhelming. You have to devote a lot of time to do this well or hire someone who is, usually, not cheap to take care of it. Even then, you will need to budget time to manage that person or vendor. It can be daunting as a full-time job, and it can set you up for failure if you are trying to control or establish systems alongside your duties as owner.

The tragedy is the **people working the most and least able to spend time on systems are the people who most desperately need systems.** The trick is to be consistent. Thirty uninterrupted minutes of focus a day, every day, are superior to doing nothing for seven days and then going crazy and working 12 hours straight on the eighth day. If you are going to manage systems yourself, slow and steady is where the money is. It also helps if you keep in mind that a fully automated, systematized business will always sell for two to three times more than the tangled mess many of you are living with today. That can be millions of dollars of profit—or equity if you are not selling—for you, as the owner.

My hero, Michael Gerber, in his book, *The E-Myth,* talks about the concept of working on your business, as opposed to working in your business. It is a simple concept to understand but can be a bear to implement. This is exactly where most business owners stumble. To get anything of value done in your business, you need to set time aside when you are not doing the work of your business, such as answering the phones, paying bills, coaching employees, and cleaning the toilet. Then, you can focus on developing your business-creating systems.

Before I leave you stressed out about the wall of work to be done, there is an answer. It's a system, a system for making systems, in fact.

SYSTEM-MAKING SYSTEM (PATENT PENDING… IN MY MIND)

1. Buy this Freaking Genius book for everyone on your team. Don't cheap out. At the very least, read them this chapter and get them on board. If your team is not on board, you are in for an uphill battle.

2. Break down your company into major and minor systems.

   a) Major would be things such as sales/marketing, fulfillment, and accounting.

   b) Minor would be smaller sub-systems that together make up each of those major processes.

3. Start with a minor, easy system.

4. Document what you are doing now. The key word here is document. It's not enough for everyone to understand it. It needs to be written down.

5. Ask a ton of questions about how you would like things to be done in the fairytale perfect future universe and what you don't love about how it is going now.

6. Document unwanted results, with the goal of eliminating them. Also, document positive outcomes. This should be done by the people directly involved in each specific step. You merely oversee or check their finished product.

7. Document System 1.0. **This will suck**, and that is okay. If you expect it to be great, you will be disappointed.

8. Implement System 1.0. Remember System 1.0 will not work, but you can't fix it until it is deployed.

9. Document all frustrations/things that are not working with the system and all deviations from the system. Get buy-in from all employees because every frustration and deviation must be documented.

10. Revise daily, at first, and then, weekly, as your system improves. These revisions will be huge at first, but after a while, the system will be pretty good and only need minor tweaks to make things run even more smoothly.

11. Once the system is running smoothly, decide when it needs its next checkup to make sure it still works well. This can be anywhere from three to twelve months, and often the checkup will be a five-minute conversation

confirming all is well in Happy System Town, with no changes needed.

In order to make systems happen in my business, I had to do the work. I had excellent people working with me, but it always seemed too much for me to get them to follow the above process without my direct intervention. If implementation and revisions seem overwhelming to those who stand to gain substantial financial and emotional benefits (you the owner), it is nearly undoable for people who get paid the same, regardless of whether they do their work the way they have always done it or change and disrupt everything they know. To get a system in place, I found the best way to manage this complication was to do the specific job I was trying to systematize and then work with the people who do that job every day.

My last business was a car dealership. The accounting in those bad boys is a wall of work, especially if you want it done right, and trust me, you do. My wife and I worked together to create an accounting system that we could turn over to employees that would free up our lives, so we could flit about the dealership as we pleased. Since we were in a business with a lot of cash movement, it was imperative to have this part of the business locked down. When we started, we did the whole hire-smart-people routine and assumed we could let them take care of everything. Since we wanted to stop doing these particular tasks, we hired people to take over, and systems were the order of the day.

The first thing we did was create a Google doc spreadsheet (my employees grew sick of hearing how cool Google docs are). The first row on the spreadsheet consisted of headings indicating each task associated with our accounting process. These included specifics: buying a car, entering expenses, flooring a car with the bank, paying off a car, and payroll. We documented, step by step, the places to go in our accounting system under that heading or column. We later expanded the spreadsheet to create the accounting manual, which reflected the process of gradual revisions required as systems evolved. Next, we created a daily checklist that had all the tasks any employee in accounting would do on a daily, weekly, and monthly basis. We planned out exactly which tasks were to be done and in which order.

Prior to beginning the systemization process, things were getting done in whatever order we felt like doing them, but one action depended upon another, so we ended up doing things out of order, which wasted time. We got the first draft done and followed it to the letter. Every time we ran into a problem, we either made a note and followed the system or, if that made no sense, we deviated from the system and made a note as to why we deviated and what we did instead. Another helpful practice was to put suggested time of day next to each activity, for example:

- ❍ 10:00–11:00 a.m.: Reconcile yesterday's bank statement
- ❍ 11:00–11:30 a.m.: Pay off flooring.
- ❍ 11:30–12:00 a.m.: Cap deals

We did this to see how long it took us to do each task and then revised the times along with the system. When we turned that set of accountabilities over to the employee, we knew how long a task should take and could hold employees accountable by eliminating the excuse of "I have too much work to do and not enough time to do it."

At first, we went over these notes and revised our checklist daily. As the system improved, we revised it less frequently, and within a couple of weeks we had a smoothly running checklist we could turn over to employees to hold them accountable and let them know exactly what was expected of them. By the time we sold our business, we had daily checklists for every employee. We turned over a well-oiled machine to the new owners who are still benefitting today from the systematization we did years ago.

I know it seems daunting, but once you get some momentum, you will find one set of systems touching other areas of your business, making the workload easier and easier as you go along. Systematizing one area of the business will help other areas before you "get to them." Once your staff is comfortable with the process, it gets light-years easier. On a final note, you will likely have some resistance from your staff and that is okay, but when you have people who just won't play ball, they have to go. Everyone has to be on the same page.

Chapter 6

MAKE IT RAIN: HOW TO BURY YOUR BUSINESS IN CUSTOMERS

"I have always believed that writing advertisements is the second most profitable form of writing. The first, of course, is ransom notes."

—Philip Dusenberry

"If you think advertising doesn't work, consider the millions of Americans that now think yogurt tastes good."

—Joe L. Whitley

Welcome to what I am guessing is going to be the most popular chapter of this book. In my nearly two decades of owning businesses and the thousands of conversations I have had with fellow business owners, invariably, **the biggest frustration and bottleneck is always around getting more customers.** If business owners had a magic wand that could change anything in their business, they would overwhelmingly use it to have ready, willing, and able customers lined up at their door. That is what we are going to cover in these next few pages. If the expectation of being able to produce customers at will doesn't get you fired up, you may have the wrong book! Having all the customers you want or need starts with your mindset. We are going to get to the practical how-to, ready-to-implement stuff, but we have to start at the beginning.

WE ARE IN THE CLIENT ACQUISITION BUSINESS

The problem with most business owners is they often think they are in the business of providing whatever product or service their company offers. Bankers think they are in the business of lending money. Auto repair facilities think they are in the business of fixing cars, and grocery stores think they are in the business of selling groceries. The truth of the matter is you are, first and foremost, in the client acquisition business. Nothing happens until somebody pulls out a wallet, hands you a credit card, signs a purchase order, gives you money, or otherwise commits to give you money.

That's the first mindset we, as business owners, need to anchor in our brains. The second issue is client acquisition is a tricky beast that falls into the "extremely important," but rarely "urgent" category of things on your to-do list. The problem is:

no paying customers = no business

Client acquisition is not urgent, because if you don't do anything to get a customer today, your nonexistent customer-to-be won't call and complain. Nothing will happen. To make matters worse, if you start working on client acquisition today, you are unlikely to have any positive result today. Most client acquisition strategies take time to develop and hone. The final indignation is that when you do put together some sort of client acquisition effort, it often is not tracked well, and you never really get the feeling that it made you any money.

The fact that getting customers is vitally important but not urgent, combined with poor tracking, bad past experiences, and the delayed gratification of creating and implementing a client acquisition system, keeps most business owners firmly stuck. They feel overwhelmed when it comes to growing their business or creating a repeatable, dependable system to bring in new clients. Paradoxically, that is the most important part of the business owner's job. I have been there. It is absolutely brutal to run a business while simultaneously creating, implementing, investing in, and revising a reliable, repeatable, client acquisition system.

Many times, business owners recognize the need to attract clients and choose to contract with a marketing firm to delegate, or at least get some help with, the client acquisition aspect of their business. While that is much better than ignoring the issue altogether, many of these marketing types are exactly that: marketing types. They went to college, got a fine, high-dollar education about branding and marketing, and they know exactly how Coca Cola and Nike manage their advertising and build their brands. They attempt to use those exact same concepts to grow their small business, which more often than not goes through the budget with less than stellar and rarely trackable results.

I am not a marketing type. I am a fellow business owner who also has a high-dollar education, acquired by hiring these marketing types and blowing tens of thousands of dollars on brand building and investments with no way to track results or figure ROI. Most advertising types' kryptonite is tracking and measurement. Their goal is to have you pay them to market, with no accountability for how much money you get back on your investment. Ask reps selling TV spots what guarantees they offer and let me know what they tell you when they stop laughing. **These guys get paid to sell advertising, not to grow your business.** Keep that in mind when taking their advice.

The first rule of any client acquisition system is if acquisition can't be tracked, it doesn't happen, no matter how popular the system is.

Social media can be a great tool, but many of the social media gurus out there are all about getting followers and "likes"; they don't understand the importance of getting dollars.

To combat this, you have to know who you are as a person, what your company is, where it stands in the marketplace, what it uniquely offers the market, and what you are trying to accomplish with your business. You have to do the work we covered in chapter 4. If you haven't done that yet, go back and work through the exercises there, as the rest of this chapter assumes you have all of that locked and loaded.

LEAD SOURCES: WHERE YOUR CUSTOMERS COME FROM

Done? Good! Let's talk lead sources. Early on in your business, you may have found a couple of lead sources that worked so well that you became comfortable and focused on them to build your business. That's fine and dandy until you want to take your business to the next level. After doing the same old same old for a long time, you may have grown to think other lead sources don't work in your business and you try to milk the same one or two sources with diminishing returns. It's a bummer.

You want to cultivate as many profitable lead sources as possible. You don't want one way to find 1,000 customers; you want 1,000 ways to find one customer. Let's say the bulk of your customers come from your sales force, as mine did for many years. What happens when your top three guys decide to go into competition with you and take your customers with them? What if you are the king of Google Adwords and Google changes the rules on you, as it is known to do periodically? What if, back in the day, you got all your business from your awesome Yellow Pages ad? What do you do when the Internet comes along and changes that entire business model? If you don't have multiple channels of customers coming in, everything you have worked for is in a precarious position. Commit some time to identifying more lead sources that you will follow up and develop. More is always better, but start with at least six. There will be some trial and error, and tweaking, but this is critical to the growth and sustainability of your business.

Before we can move on to how to grow your business, you will need to be clear on where you are going to take your business and what your personal goals are. "Grow my business" is not a goal. "Sell $1.2 million in gross sales with $175,000 in net profit in the next 12 months" is a goal.

Remember that if you can't track it, you aren't going to do it. You need to have goals to hold against the results of your efforts so you'll know when your efforts and systems are working. The rest of this chapter is extremely actionable, but the steps you take depend on your goals. Sketch out what you want your business to look like. Have some fun. Use the next two pages to write out your life exactly as you would like it to be, with no thought of what is and is not possible. Enjoy and dream. Then, explore more specific, actionable goals. I'll grab lunch, and we can meet back here in 20.

REVENUE:

One Year: Two Years:

Five Years: Ten Years:

NET PROFIT:

One Year: Two Years:

Five Years: Ten Years:

HOURS WORKED:

This Year: Next Year:

Five Years: Ten Years:

WEEKS OF VACATION:

This Year: Next Year:

Five Years: Ten Years:

OTHER PERSONAL GOALS:

Welcome back. My wife just made me a lovely shrimp salad, and I am fueled up and ready to get you rocking. Your next step is to create your client acquisition budget that will fuel the goals you just set. First, we need to discuss how much you are willing and able to spend to acquire customers. Many business owners cheap out here and try to get customers for the least amount possible. The problem comes when they limit themselves to, and are satisfied with, only the cheapest methods. If you can get a customer, using one strategy for $10 and another for $20, but your profit on both customers is $50, don't shut down your $20 client-acquisition strategy—it is still profitable. Use them both.

Many business owners fail to take into consideration the lifetime value of a customer and only consider the initial purchase value of the customer when deciding their client acquisition budget. Repeat customers are cheaper to keep than new customers are to acquire, and that doesn't even take referrals into account. Many a savvy business owner has built a monster business on spending 100% of their initial profit on acquiring that customer. Sounds counter intuitive, but if you can build a 10,000 strong customer base with effectively no marketing costs—you are on to something...

Don't fall for bad thinking here. "I don't have the money to market" is deadly. You don't have the money because you need more clients. You need more clients because you don't have enough money. This is circular logic you have to kill. It will not serve you or your business. That said, some methods of client acquisition are less expensive than others. You can get started on the cheap ones, but you will trade time for money. The less money you have available, the more time you will need to allocate to client acquisition. Speaking engagements take a lot of time, because you must find the audience, prepare your speech and materials, make your presentation, and follow up with the prospective clients that you just spoke to. That, my friend, is a lot of time and effort. It is also very effective and nearly free. There are no right or wrong answers here. It is really a function of your personal and business goals and what you enjoy doing.

Back to creating your client acquisition budget: the only money truly at risk is the capital you invest in the trial-and-error process of figuring out what works for you. This is where finding a qualified consultant, mastermind group, or mentor can mitigate that risk. Once you get streamlined and systematized, every dollar you spend should bring back many dollars in return. Once you have this nailed down, your marketing budget is only limited to the amount of work your business can handle. Here is a simplified example to show you what I mean:

$1 per click to your website

100 clicks = $100

10 percent of clicks become customers

10 percent conversion = 10 new customers

$100 for clicks divided by 10 customers =
each customer costs $10

average customer from pay per click
advertising spends $42

cost to deliver product/service = $12

$42 new revenue: $12 cost of product/ service = $30 gross profit

$30 gross profit: $10 to acquire said client = $20 to your bottom line

$10 investment in pay per click = $20 in profit (assuming new customer never spends another dollar with you)

In that scenario, how much can you spend on that channel (Adwords) for client acquisition? You can spend as much as you want, assuming you can deliver enough of your product or service. It's straightforward, but I am guessing you are not there just yet for a few reasons:

1. You don't know your lead source for all of your customers.
2. You don't know the cost of that lead source.
3. You don't know the conversion percent of each advertising channel you use.
4. You don't know your average client spend *per lead source.*
5. You don't know your cost to deliver that product/service.

Since many of you don't yet have systems in place to generate that data, you are going to have to create them alongside your client acquisition systems. You may not know what lead sources work and don't work. In that case, you might have to go through many different media, including pay per click, direct mail, events, trade shows, print ads, radio, and TV, before you can get an optimized customer source. You may have to explore different variations on those themes—such as what you say in your advertising copy, the offers you make, the lists you mail to, graphic design, and how you follow up—to find a source that is reliably profitable. Once you have this all figured out, you will have a system of multiple, dependable ways to predictably grow your business. It can be scary, but the result is growth at whatever pace you decide.

You will have to commit some amount of money to your client acquisition budget. I recommend a percentage of sales. Between 5 and 10 percent is a good starting point, depending on the structure of your business. The key is to use a fixed percentage as you grow. It will train you and your staff early on to have client acquisition as an investment that automatically grows as your business grows. Your business will benefit from the magic formula below:

More marketing = more sales. More sales = more marketing. Repeat.

When you make your budget, you have to be comfortable with the fact that you are going to blow money on things that don't work. You can mitigate this risk by working with people who know what they are doing in their field and ruthlessly, mercilessly track. Remember, many of the people trying to sell you advertising will not be fans of tracking, because their goal is for you to spend money with them and growing your business is a bonus in their eyes. They will try to "enlighten" you on the benefits of name recognition, brand building, and the like. These are all nice, but for a small business, they must be bonuses to actual ROI.

I would love to give you recommendations on what sort of client acquisition strategies are best for you, but it would be irresponsible of me to do that without knowing you and your business. This is one of my favorite areas to help grow businesses, so feel free to contact me for help if you run into a wall. If I don't have availability or my rates don't fit your budget, I will be happy to turn you on to someone far less fun and attractive but nearly as capable. The point is to make a budget.

THE CUSTOMER ACQUISITION CALENDAR

Next up, we'll discuss the customer acquisition calendar. This is one of the simplest yet least utilized tasks I see in businesses. The key to getting clients to recognize you, care about you, and ultimately spend money with you is consistency. Granted, consistency can be a weak spot for many of us A-types, get-'er-done business owners. Your customer acquisition calendar will compensate for our natural wandering off toward shiny objects. It will represent all of the things that need to get done in the next 12 months to hit your sales and profit goals. No, you can't wait until January 1 to make one.

Notice I didn't say the calendar would have all of the things that *you* are going to do. It has all of the things that need to get done. Delegate tasks. Here are a few examples you might put on your calendar to get the blood flowing:

- Write, print, and send (all three of these tasks would be on different dates) a monthly newsletter to all customers and prospects.
- Get one speaking gig per month in front of ideal clients.
- Cold-call your 10 largest customers who haven't bought in six months.

- Design and write copy for a postcard.
- Learn full capabilities of CRM system and build new marketing campaign.
- Read a book like this one to get fresh ideas and then implement them.
- Book a restaurant for customer appreciation event.
- Write an e-mail auto responder series requesting referrals, thanking customers for purchases, up-selling, and so on.
- Write copy for lead generation tool and give it away on your website in exchange for customer email/ info.
- Video customer testimonials for website, proposals, blog, and the like.
- Interview your top five customers on video to find out why they do business with you and who else out there is like them. Make them feel special.
- Write a weekly blog and guest post on industry rock stars' blogs.
- Record a weekly podcast.
- Send salespeople to sales training.
- Record the on-hold message for phone system, telling people about your newest product offering and your core values.

This list is far from comprehensive but should give you some ideas and build some excitement. There are a ton of things that you can do to attract clients, but they are usually the first to get pushed off to the side when the inevitable "fire" needs to be put out in your business. So, having a client acquisition calendar and committing to it is huge. When you take **consistent action over extended periods of time**, you will be amazed at the results that cumulative effort produces.

Okay, who is up for a rant on consistency? No one? Great! You may have noticed that a theme has been developing in these pages, and that theme is consistency! Each of the concepts in this book require consistent and persistent action. Virtually none of them will work if you dabble or give them a try and then move on to the next thing. You will always have better luck taking on fewer initiatives and seeing them through to fruition than starting on a bunch of stuff much of which fizzles and ends. Remember a poor plan executed well beats a perfect plan left unexecuted, every time. Consistency! Rant over.

Listing all the things you need to do to hit your goals over the next year can feel overwhelming. When you break it down to two to five weekly tasks that take 30–60 minutes each over the span of a year, it doesn't seem so insurmountable. Once you get in the habit of following the calendar, you will wonder how you ever lived without it.

Each item on your calendar will have projected revenue associated with it. If you meet or exceed that revenue, ramp up that activity. If you don't meet it but are getting some response, tweak it. If it is an absolute bust, dump it and replace it. You must replace it and not just dump it, or you will be back where you started, relying on the same one, two, or three methods of bringing in customers. Make sure you plan an entire year out. Revisit the calendar monthly, but you need a baseline to know what the plan is if you wish to make intelligent changes to it. Once more, the key is tracking and consistency. Keep these old calendars and notes, even when the year is over. It can be a ton of fun to look over old calendars and remember where you came from. You can also revisit ideas that didn't work then but might make sense now.

Let's touch on sales and salespeople. No matter how many client acquisition strategies you have working for you, unless yours is a totally online business, you are going to have salespeople. Salespeople can be great; they can also be a ton of work, expensive, and time consuming. Sales management can suck the life out of you if this is not your natural talent. Your client acquisition calendar is an excellent tool for lowering your dependence on salespeople.

Salespeople who generate leads, sell to those leads, and maintain the leads as customers may feel their customers should go with them when they leave your company. To combat this, have your client acquisition system centralized and automated with systematized, perfected corporate messaging. There are a ton of opportunities for you to communicate with your prospects and customers:

- Lead generation
- Facebook posts, tweets, blogs, etc.
- Thank-you's to customers for their purchases

- Messages to customers (e.g., "We noticed you haven't purchased in a while.")
- Thank-you's to prospective customers for requesting product information
- Monthly newsletters
- Interviews with employees and other experts in the field
- Requests for reviews, referrals, and testimonials
- Up-selling
- Birthday/anniversary greetings
- Special sales

The options are limitless! Your clients should be getting your culture, your core values, and USP from many different types of media at many different stages in their buying cycle. This kind of communication also positions them as consumers who come to you to buy, as opposed to your salespeople going to them to sell. People love to buy, but they hate to be sold. Systematizing your prospect and client communications with intentional, well-written copy makes sure your message goes out consistently every time, regardless of the quality of your salespeople or what kind of day they are having.

Hopefully, by now, you have put together a plan to bring in the customers you need to reach your goals. Once you get customers coming in regularly, there is one more potential business killer that is lurking in the shadows and that I don't want to leave unaddressed.

CASH FLOW

Lack of cash flow has taken out more businesses than any other factor so we need to touch on this topic before we move on. You may wonder why I bring this up in the middle of a chapter about client acquisition, but there is a good reason. Most cash-flow problems are actually customer acquisition problems. Depending on the type of business you are in, and your business model, the arrival of new customers by the boatload can actually be a giant cash suck. This is especially true if you offer payment terms or have an overhead/capital-intensive business. I want to make sure none of you:

a) Refuse to embark on growing your business because of cash constraints;

b) Embark on growing your business, have success, and then have to stop due to cash constraints.

Many businesses I have worked with feel cash flow is an outside entity over which they have no control. They may think that's just how it's done in their business, they just have a lot of receivables, or getting paid in 90 days is industry standard, and there is nothing they can do about it. This is not an accurate or helpful way to think.

These attitudes can literally take a business down. For years, I had government contracts and got paid 30–90 days after I delivered the product and begged for my money. I was told and believed, "That's just how they pay." Truth is these claims are rarely reality or the whole story. I found certain government buyers actually had credit cards for certain types of purchases. They could use them any time, with no waiting. I also discovered many government entities are required by law to take advantage of early pay opportunities, for example, 3 percent 10, net 30, which means they get a 3 percent discount for paying within 10 days or can pay the full amount in 30 days. I use the government as an example because governments are known for being notoriously slow payers. It is likely your customers are able to pay more quickly.

If you are running a $6M business, that is $500K per month in sales. If you are getting paid, on average, within 45 days, that is $750K in receivables. You can pay neither rent nor payroll with receivables, because they require cash. If you could move your customers to paying at the time the product or service is delivered, or negotiate a 50 percent deposit upon order, with the balance due at delivery, you could instantly improve your cash position by nearly $1,000,000. There is a tremendous amount of value your company can squeeze out of $1M with newfound cash hanging around.

YOU CHOOSE WHOM YOU DO BUSINESS WITH!

You may still be convinced your customers will never pay on time or with a deposit. Have you asked them? Have you offered them a discount? If you have and they refuse to pay, I still have great news for you. You get to pick your customers.

Let's take doctors, for example, who are paid by insurance companies. Insurance companies are the worst payers known to man. No problem. Doctors could target affluent customers who want personalized care and premium service more than they want to use their insurance company. They could limit their practice to 200 patients and charge each of their 200 exclusive patients

$10,000 annually for premier personalized service, house calls, and on-demand consults. Since the average family doctor has over 2,000 patients, in addition to being able to provide much better service, doctors who adopt this system work fewer hours and make a ton more money.

In this example, the doctors changed their cash position from hundreds of thousands of dollars tied up with the insurance company to $2 million paid in advance at the beginning of the year. Not to mention they get to choose the patients they want to work with and they rid their life of the insurance companies altogether. However, 200 patients aren't going to show up magically, but with an average of 2,000 patients per doctor, annually, if the doctors offer this type of service to their 2,000 patients and get a measly 5 percent response rate, they are already halfway there. For the other half, it's back to the client acquisition calendar.

That is the beauty of taking charge of the client acquisition process in your business. You have control over how many customers come to you, what type of customers they are, and once they aren't so scarce, fun options appear before your very eyes.

If your competitors haven't put together client attraction systems, don't track their spending, don't understand the concept of budgeting to get customers, and spend little to no money to acquire new customers and are not consistent they won't be able to compete with you spending well researched, consistent, effective dollars. **The one who can spend the MOST to attract a new client wins!**

Take charge. Be proactive. Decide how many customers you need to achieve your goals. Create a budget and plan to attract those customers. Put it into action. Tweak as you go and don't look back.

Chapter 7

THE ONLY THREE WAYS TO GROW YOUR BUSINESS

"Nothing is particularly hard if you divide it into small jobs."

—Henry Ford

"Capital isn't scarce; vision is."

—Sam Walton

This chapter is going to be short, punchy, and full of actionable genius, so hold on to your hats! I had been a business owner for a decade before I was exposed to the concept that there were only three ways to grow a business. The ideas were so clear and simple I was a little pissed off I hadn't heard them before or put them together on my own.

The first way to grow your business is also the most obvious: get more customers. As key to your success as customers are, getting more of them is expensive and there is no leverage. It's much harder to get 100 new customers than it is to employ the other two ways to grow your business. If you want to make twice as much money next year as this year, you have to get approximately twice as many customers, assuming you don't use either of the two other ways to grow your business.

Adding new customers is the lifeblood of your business, and the other two ways depend on having existing customers, so customers must be gained, or maintained, on a consistent basis. Magic happens when you do all three business-growing activities simultaneously. We covered a ton of ways to get new customers in chapter 6 and will do so again in chapter 10, so I am just going to briefly outline my favorite way to get new customers here.

CREATE A REFERRAL SYSTEM

If you have been in business any length of time, you have probably heard how important referrals are and you may already be turning off your brain or considering skipping ahead. The problem is referrals really are important and few business owners have created a strong referral system.

There can be negative energy around referrals. Business owners and employees are often too shy to ask for them and don't have a system built around acquiring referrals. When business owners hear some jerk like me banging the referral drum, they figure it wouldn't work in their business and move on with their life, referral-free, hoping referrals just wander in on their own. That makes for a sad day indeed.

The good news is referrals are just like anything else. Once you create and implement a system and foster a referral culture in your company, they keep coming in with almost no ongoing work on your part.

Although I could write an entire book on just this subject, I am going to limit our time here to a Freaking Genius list, packed with a ton of actionable ideas, and let you sort through them. Don't fall for the temptation to scroll through these without action. There are a couple of ideas here that stand alone and could double your business. See if you can find 'em.

- If your product or service is subpar, fix it before you start asking for referrals.
- Be outrageous, be different, and be yourself. The stronger your culture and core values are, the more referrals will come. You will be the only one who does what you do, in the way that you do it. Like-minded people tend to cluster and refer others, so you end up creating one raving fan who refers you to the next one, and so on, into eternity.
- When a sale fails, seek feedback. Ask for referrals even from people who don't buy. Ask them why they didn't buy, ask how you can improve, and ask whom they know who could benefit from your product or service.
- Be careful about offering money, rewards, and gifts. I found my best referrers sometimes refer less when there is money involved. They feel the person they want to refer will find out about the money and think less of them and their referral. If you are going to give money

or a prize, make sure the person referred, as well as the referrer, gets a reward. That way, they both win and feel good about life.

- Make it fun to refer to you. Send an unadvertised prize to the referrer after the referral. Recognize top referrers in e-mails, newsletters, and pictures on the wall of your business.
- Have contests. Which employee can get the most referrals? Which customer? Which non-customer?
- Create strategic partnerships in which you create joint ventures with someone who sells to your customers but does not compete with you. An example would be a jeweler doing a joint venture with a wedding planner. The jeweler sends a letter to his customers, offering a special discount on the wedding planner's services and vice versa. This is a fine way to get dozens of referrals in one shot.
- Provide your referrers the tools they need to refer you, including web pages, full lists of services, brochures, the right phone number, or a personalized sales rep to whom they can refer others.
- Give special services and bonuses to referred customers and their referees.
- Have quarterly events and invite only referrers and referees.

- Create a list of your 100 dream customers. Ask your current customers if anyone has a contact specifically to that person or company.

There are tons and tons more, but that should get your creative juices flowing and put you well on your way to implementing a referral system.

INCREASE SALES FREQUENCY

The second way to grow your business is to increase the frequency with which your customers purchase your product. There are a couple of ways to do this: the easy way and the hard way. The hard way is still an excellent way to grow your business. There is a ton of ways to get people to buy more often:

- Send them a birthday card and offer a free upgrade or birthday special. You can supercharge this with half birthdays, along with family members' birthdays, or even birthdays of people they have referred. You just want to be in front of them as often as possible.
- Send them a card on the anniversary date of when they first became your customer.
- Organize special preferred-customer-only sales and events.
- Do seasonal promotions: We always liked smaller holidays that no one else advertised, such as Chinese New Year, Mothers Day, Groundhog Day, and Kwanzaa. Customers thought these were a blast.

- Huge events, including tent sales, conferences, and customer appreciation events can encourage additional purchases.

- Make sure your customers know about all the products you offer; perhaps highlight a certain product or service every month.

- Send out an informational newsletter to every one of your customers and, ideally, to your entire list of prospects as well.

The easy way to get your customers to buy from you more frequently is to create a product or service your customer will pay for on a monthly basis, for example, a "club" that your customer can belong to. Before you start to protest that your product lasts forever and your customers only need it when they need it, let me tell you I have been there. I owned a car dealership. People, on average, buy a car every four years. How on earth could I sell them a monthly club? There are plenty of ways, such as lifetime oil changes, paid for upfront. I get to see my customers and their car every three months and have the opportunity to inspect the car for service work that needs to be done. That can be worth more than the initial profit I made on the sale of the car. I could also charge them a monthly fee to have their car washed weekly and waxed every couple of months. That comes with a monthly fee and the benefit of having them wander around my lot to see what's new, while they wait for us to detail their car. I could set up an offer that ensures if they trade vehicles every two years with me, as opposed to every four years with any other dealer, they get an amazing price for their trade, along with other free service upgrades.

Jewelers have picked up on this; some offer free ring cleanings for life. They ensure their customers come in periodically and browse the store while their ring is cleaned. Lawyers offer monthly programs for which their clients pay a monthly fee. When their clients need legal services, they already have banked hours with their attorney. Look for ways you can turn your onetime purchase into a monthly product or service. There are 1,000 ways to skin this cat, and you can make it happen in your business!

Author's note: no cats were harmed in the making of this book.

INCREASE THE DOLLAR AMOUNT OF AN AVERAGE SALE

The third and final (not to mention my all-time favorite) way to grow your business is to increase the dollar amount of your average sale. Another one you can do the easy way or the hard way. The hard way is to package goods, perhaps with a discount, give a free prize (think makeup counter at Macy's) if your customers spend a certain amount with you, or offer a loyalty program in which they get their tenth order free.

Don't forget about up-sells. A famous example of a functional up-sell is the "Would you like to supersize that?" fast-food tactic. As soon as your customer buys one thing, offer him a second product or service that goes well with the first. These are all excellent ways to incrementally grow your business.

Now, for the easy way, and don't be fooled by its simplicity. Without overstating it, these three words can easily bring you 1,000 times the amount you paid for this book: ***raise your prices.***

This is my all-time favorite business strategy. The secret sauce in this option is when you get a new customer, there are acquisition costs and the cost of the product or service you provide. When you raise your prices, it's all profit. Let's look at the numbers:

- Assume you currently have 1,000 customers who each spend $1,000 per year, for a total of $1,000,000 in revenue.
- Let's say your cost of goods, not including marketing, is 50 percent, or $500K, and your overhead is 40 percent, or $400K.
- $1,000,000 - $500,000 - $400,000 = $100,000 annual profit.
- To double your income, you would need to double your customers. You might get some economies of scale on your overhead, but that usually goes up with your customer count.

Now let's check out how what happens to your profit when you raise your prices 20 percent.

- Income per customer goes to $1,200 X 1,000 customers = $1,200,000.
- Cost of goods sold holds firm at $500K and your overhead is still $400K.
- $1,200,000 - $500,000 - $400,000 = $300,000, or **a 300% increase in your annual profit with only a 20 percent bump in price!**

- Even if you lose 10 percent of your customers over the price raise, the math still works.
- $1,080,000 (900 customers X $1,200) - $540,000 - $400,000 = $140,000. This is still a 40 percent increase in profit with 10 percent less customers and 10 percent less work.

I know it can be scary to raise prices; I have been there, friend, but it is truly the easiest way to grow profit. That doesn't even take into account the added bonuses of being able to spend more to acquire new customers, being able to serve your customers better, and give a better guarantee! More profit opens all sorts of doors for your business.

If you are still hell bent against making a buck and too scared to raise your prices, at the very least create a "premium version" of your product and sell that for more money. You won't get any customer complaints, and you will often be shocked at how some subset of your customer base is always going to buy the most expensive thing available because that's who they are. Help that man out and give him something expensive to buy!

If you already have a premium product, make another and turn your first premium product into your "middle" product. If you don't think you can make a premium product, let's use our friends the credit card companies as an example. Banks wanted another way to lend money, so they developed charge cards that charged interest for the use of their money. Then, they came up with the bright idea of an annual fee of $50–$100 for the privilege of having their card. Just when you think there is nowhere else to go, American Express comes out with the Platinum card.

That bad boy has an annual fee of around $500. Amex had such good luck with the Platinum card they came out with the Black (Centurion) card, with a $10,000 price tag just for the privilege of having it. They position it well. They do zero advertising. It is purchased by invitation only, and customers can only qualify by spending somewhere between $250K and $500K in a year. People literally line up to pay $10,000 to have Amex's premium product. Customers intentionally spend as much as they can just to get the invite. Amex makes even more money partnering with those who offer high-end goods for their specialized list of customers. What premium products can you create?

If you have been counting along as we go, you may have noticed we have gone over all three strategies, but in the spirit of always trying to over deliver, here are a couple of little bonus items that can supercharge those three ways to grow your business.

Try providing an irresistible offer. This should go hand in hand with your USP. Once you know your customers' unique pain, and how you alone can uniquely fix it for them, an irresistible offer is right around the corner. Build your case in such a way that any reasonable person would think only a fool would pass up this deal.

The best way to make your offer more irresistible is to take away the customer's risk. A money-back guarantee is the minimum standard of performance. I am so committed to my Freaking Genius clients that if they don't hit the goals we set out for them, I buy them a cruise for two in exchange for wasting their time. Do you see how that takes away the risk? Be creative, and put your money where your mouth is.

The last piece of the supercharger pie is to be different. If it's in your wheelhouse, go for it and be outrageous! This works not only with your irresistible offer but also with your guarantee. Which makes you more excited to buy, the offer of a 100 percent money-back guarantee, or "If you aren't 100 percent satisfied, you can get your money back and slap my face, guaranteed"? Too much? Here are some examples that are more moderate in their conditions:

- No questions asked, you get a 100 percent money-back guarantee, for any reason, no matter how crazy.
- "We *refuse* to accept your money until you are deliriously happy with us!"

Have some fun, get creative, and come up with one that fits your business. You may or may not like the title, *I'm a Freaking Genius*, but you will dang well remember it. Outrageous = unforgettable. It also leads to fun. Fun leads to happy employees, customers, and business owners. Don't take my word for it when you can get out there and get outrageous!

Part Three:

LET'S TALK ABOUT PEOPLE

"When my boss asked me who the stupid one was, me or him, I told him everyone knows he doesn't hire stupid people."

—Anonymous

"Clothes make the man. Naked people have little or no influence on society."

—Mark Twain

Chapter 8

SALES...AND PEOPLE... AND SALESPEOPLE

"There are worse things in life than death. Have you ever spent an evening with an insurance salesman?"

—Woody Allen

In our discussion of sales and salespeople, we are going to move fast, and you are going to have way too many actionable items for a single person. Heads will spin, and you might get a little dizzy. Consider yourself warned.

If you are a business owner, you are a salesperson. I hear business owners all of the time bellyache about how they hate sales, can't sell, or don't want to sell. Tough jerky. If you are a business owner and want employees, you have to sell them on coming to work for you, as opposed to working elsewhere, or staying home and watching *Seinfeld* reruns. Once they come aboard, it is your responsibility to sell them on the idea of putting forward their best effort every day. It's your job to sell vendors on taking care of you, convince investors their capital is safe with you, and persuade customers and employees your business is worthy of their time, money, and passion.

BUSINESS OWNER = GOOD SALESPERSON

Taking that into consideration, the skill of selling and persuasion is a craft that will serve you your whole life, in just about any area of life where you contend with other humans. Want a date? Sell your good looks, charisma, and clean criminal record. Want your kid to pick up his room, stay in school, say no to drugs, and salute as you enter a room? That's a sales job too. Want the nice lady behind the car rental desk to upgrade you for free? Sure would be handy to know how to sell that idea to her. Want to hold salespeople accountable for specific performance? The best salesperson is going to win that battle, shouldn't it be you?

Not being able to sell, as a business owner, is like not being able to read as a student. You might be able to get by, but it won't be pretty. Selling done right is all about understanding and ultimately, serving people. Selling skills affect not only your ability to sell but also your ability to interact successfully with people both inside and outside your business.

Just like everything else in your business, selling is a process that can and should be systematized. The concepts that govern how you sell a pair of shoes are the same set of concepts you use to sell the idea of a second date with someone you like. We are going to have some fun in this chapter and apply these concepts not only to your work as a business owner but also to success in your personal life. The big takeaway is these concepts work when interacting with other human beings, regardless of circumstance.

Let's start with your business. Most salespeople act as if there were an infinite number of objections, or reasons that people don't buy, so they wing it when objections surface feeling that they have to come up with a custom response to one of the infinite number of objections.

Here is an enlightening exercise. Sit down with your sales team members and have them yell out every objection they've ever received. Write those objections on a whiteboard at the front of the room. They will lose steam after about a dozen objections, and rarely will you reach two dozen. Eliminate all of the duplicate answers. "Your prices are too high," and "I can't afford it," are really the same objections. You will find there are only three to six objections that cover 98–100 percent of the reasons people don't buy.

Next, have all your salespeople come up with their best way to overcome each objection. Write what they say on the whiteboard next to the objection. Don't limit this to what your salespeople think they should say in a selling situation. Expand it to what you, as the business owner, can do to eliminate or negate that objection, or work together with your sales team on issues they can't change alone. Your salespeople could have a lot of concerns. Some you yourself will have to solve. Others your salespeople may need to handle on their own, and many you will work on together. Some examples are:

Objection: The price is too high.

Potential fix: Build value through marketing material. Work with your salespeople to create the materials and explore how to build value. Enhance your offering to have a higher perceived value

Potential fix: Create a lower-priced option. This is something you handle.

Potential fix: Bring up the subject of price earlier in the sales process. The salesperson should have done this.

Potential fix: Take the time to uncover the prospects' pain, another responsibility of the salesperson.

Potential fix: Work with customers who have less price sensitivity. This is something you and the salespeople can address by changing the marketing message and where you market.

This is a great opportunity for another rant. I run into a lot of business owners who feel that their customers would never pay "that kind of money" for their service or their customers don't have "that kind of money." The beauty of it is that you own the place, you are in charge, and you can choose any customer you like! Most business owners choose customers who make and spend money in amounts similar to what the business owner makes and spends, and if the business owner would "never spend that kind of money," they believe their customers wouldn't spend that kind of money. They do this not because of strategic genius but merely because of comfort level. The crazy thing is there is less competition for the low-spending customer than the affluent. How many Wal-Mart ads do you see in comparison with Neiman Marcus ads or Ford ads in comparison with Lamborghini ads?

Still don't think your customer will "pay that kind of money," or "I am not in a business that has high line products"? How about car washes for a boring price-sensitive example? Ultimate Shine Car wash charges $150,000 for a car wash. How about the kitchen sink? It's hard to get too expensive with sinks. Check Blido, which sells its premier sink for $80,000. Let's do one more: headphones. I got my pair for free with my iPhone, but you can go all the way up to $300 for a pair of Beats by Dr. Dre. Still not impressed? How about the Colorware Illusion version for $1,000? How about the Crystal Rocked Swarovski Glamour series for $2,650? Whatever your product or service, someone is charging at least ten times more than what you are charging.

I know those are extreme examples and those companies may sell a limited number of those high-priced options. Even if that is the case—which it rarely is—what do you think having those high-priced items does to the sales of their entry-level prices? Even if you never sell a single one of your premium offerings with their astronomical price tags, merely having them available can do wonders for your status in the eyes of your customers and prospects.

Enough ranting. Moving on ...

When coordinated changes are made, starting at the salesperson level and working with marketing and management, magic happens.

Once all your salespeople have given optimal responses to each objection, go through them, as a group. Take the best aspects of each idea, and put together the two to three ways to overcome common objections they hear day in and day out. Record these in your sales manual (remember chapter 5?). From that day forward, that will be how everyone at your company responds to that objection creating a fantastic baseline for every salesperson!

Finally, have the salespeople role-play in groups of three. One is "buying," one is "selling," and one is observing. Have the buyer use the objections you just came up with and the seller respond with the agreed-upon best responses. Afterward, have each person share the experience from his/her unique perspective as buyer, salesperson, and observer. Make sure every salesperson participates in this exercise and practices dealing with every objection from all three perspectives. Salespeople love to "practice" in front of customers. Have them "practice" like this with you on a weekly basis because it can be extremely powerful.

Often salespeople resist "selling" in front of you and each other, but at times, it is non-negotiable, and must be done. The adoption rate of your new best practice for overcoming objections will skyrocket with routine practice. Take advantage of muscle memory. When your salespeople actually say the words in a non-stressful, nonthreatening environment, they will find those same words coming out of their mouths comfortably on sales calls. Instead of winging it, they should only be using the "best" response.

KEEP YOUR CUSTOMER COMFORTABLE

Now we will talk about some stuff that is more about psychology than sales and is a ton of fun. The first rule of selling sounds simple but is often overlooked. Make sure the person you are trying to help with your product or service is comfortable, or ideally, downright happy! Uncomfortable people want only to become comfortable. The easiest way for them to do this is to get rid of the person or thing they believe is making them uncomfortable. People, as a rule, do not like to part with money. If you, or a member of your sales team, are with them at a time when they fear they might spend money, they will likely get rid of the perceived problem: you. That tends to have a negative effect on sales.

It is up to you to make sure they are comfortable. Never come off as knowing everything or try to show them how smart you are. That is a total rookie move that makes customers feel that they don't have the knowledge you have, and you are going to take advantage of them. It can also lead to anger and frustration. Using insider industry words, slang, or abbreviations the customer may not be familiar with is a great way to make people feel stupid and want to get away from you. Do everything you can to make sure your customers are comfortable and on a par with you. "How the heck am I supposed to take charge of another person's feelings?" you ask. That is a fine question, which brings me to the next exciting concept in sales.

TAKE RESPONSIBILITY FOR EVERYTHING

You must take responsibility for everything. When customers don't buy, it's human nature to believe those customers were in a bad mood when they arrived, didn't have the money, or were just jerks.

That might be the case. Maybe they did come to the meeting in a terrible mood, and maybe they were jerks. The problem is, at the end of the day, customers who don't buy don't get the benefit of your product or service. You don't get the benefit of payment for your time. You can't control how they feel before they meet with you, but you can greatly influence how they feel during your meeting. Feel free to call out their bad attitude and give them space to be open. If you are getting a negative vibe, don't pretend it isn't there. Ask a grumpy customer, "Hey Mike, I have heard great things about you, but you don't seem to be following me. Is everything okay? Would it be easier to move our meeting to a better time for you?"

Rarely will Mike bite your head off or reschedule. Usually, he will appreciate your being real with him. This question gives him space to realize his attitude and acknowledge you understand him and care about him, and he is more likely to reply, "Sorry. I had a bad day, but I do want to figure this out. Let's keep going."

A more advanced concept is to let the grumpy customers "save" you. Act as if you are struggling. Fumble, or ask for their help or opinion. I've even seen sales guys stumble, or drop an item. All of these tactics encourage your prospective customers to come to the rescue, which allows them to feel good and get their mind off their problems. You will come across as a regular guy instead of the intimidating guy who knows everything and is going to take customers' money. This can be uncomfortable for veteran salespeople who feel they know everything and are hell bent on proving it to the world. This ties in nicely with my core value "Be Real". People are more comfortable with regular human beings that make mistakes than with slick, polished fake salespeople. Decide if the goal of a sales call is to feel smart and important or to help customers purchase your product or service. If it is the latter, focus on making the prospect, not yourself, feel smart and important.

You are in charge of the outcome. Every time the outcome is not a sale, don't fall into the poor man's trap of justifying failure with reasons denying it was your fault. Take the time to review what you could and should have done better. **SWSWSW: Some will, some won't, so what!** You can't make everyone buy, but you can do your best to make sure you learn from your mistakes and give your best, most skilled effort to help every prospect.

NEXT FREAKING GENIUS CONCEPT: LET THEM COME TO YOU.

Get comfortable making statements such as "Maybe we are not a fit," and "It doesn't sound like this is going to work for you." Oftentimes, salespeople are so afraid of the "no" that they don't give the prospect the space and freedom to voice his or her concerns. Those concerns must be overcome to make the sale, and they must be uncovered before they can be overcome. You have got to lean into the uncomfortable space and let the customer tell you what he or she thinks. Once you get used to that, it is actually much easier than trying to bully people into doing what you want.

Picture yourself in a conversation with someone who keeps inching closer and closer into your personal space. Your immediate reaction is to back off or get the heck out of the room. That is exactly how prospects feel. Now, picture the person you are talking with leaning back and speaking softly and quietly. You will lean in and strain to hear. If you are standing together, talking, and the person you are talking with turns and walks down the hall while speaking, you will follow him. Let people come to you. They love to buy, but they hate to be sold.

The last piece to this puzzle is confidence, yet another feature that works amazingly well with people of the opposite sex. People can smell the stink of desperation from a mile away, and they don't want any part of it. If you are on a sales call, interview, or in any interaction with fellow homo sapiens, and they get a whiff of your desperation, they won't be able to get out of there fast enough. On the other hand, if your prospects feel you don't need the sale, and you are there to make sure their needs are met, they are free to buy and feel it was their decision. This is where you want to be, where your customers do not feel pushed into making a decision. This is much more comfortable. It wipes out buyers' remorse, returns, and people backing out of deals.

Let's talk about pain. You are going to love pain! Why?

No pain = no sale

Big pain = big, easy sale

SELLING TO YOUR CUSTOMERS' PAIN

If you are a doctor, who do you think is going to be a tougher sell, the guy who has a slight cough or the guy whose arm is held on with duct tape and willpower? Good salespeople spend their time seeking the guy with duct tape, not badgering Mr. Slight Cough.

The best way to do this is to ask questions that hit the guy in pain right between the eyes. You can do this in written marketing materials. For example, which one of these headlines will get your customers' attention faster: "On sale now: accounting software that puts you in control," or "Tired of your employees robbing you blind?"

Ask a question that will make customers jump up, raise their hand, and scream, "That's me!" Which do you think will get more response:

"Most Courteous Pest Control in California," or "Do you want to risk your family being covered in creepy crawly bed bugs?"

Ask the question that sticks a hot iron right into their eye socket to get their attention. You can do this in print, or in person.

Good salespeople move as quickly as possible from a boring, low-energy conversation to a passionate, pain-focused conversation. You can't fix customers' problems until they realize how bad their situation is.

Pain = profit (period).

Face-to-face meetings benefit from questions such as "How long has this been a problem?" "On a scale from one to ten, how important is it that you get this taken care of?" "What has stopped you from getting this handled so far?" "What is your budget to get this taken care of?"

These are all questions to help gauge the prospects' commitment to addressing the problem. If it has been a problem for the last eight months, it's probably not that big a problem. If they have not considered a budget to address the problem, that also indicates it is likely a minor problem.

NEVER UNDERESTIMATE THE POWER OF A LITTLE OUTRAGEOUSNESS

People are sick of normal because they are bombarded with vanilla sales pitches all day. Good salespeople stand out. Even the most boring, uptight industry known to man, the insurance business, is getting in on the action. Did you ever think you would see a gecko hawking car insurance? How about Allstate, and the "Mayhem" guy? What about this peach of a book you are reading now? Be different, be outrageous, or be gone. Break through the noise of your prospects' day and jolt them into attention. This can and should be a ton of fun if you let your creative juices flow and be yourself. Today's world is insanely politically correct, with so many companies following the last boring guy. It is so easy to stand out and have fun, and it is a lot easier if you did the work in chapter 4 and have a clear set of core values you ooze from every pore, along with a rock-solid, Freaking Genius, compelling USP.

It can take years to get good with these concepts, but I want you to be aware of them and have the opportunity to initiate the ones that make sense to you. Ignore the ones you aren't feeling positive about.

Let's move on to salespeople in your business and the dynamics surrounding them. Oftentimes, salespeople are the most highly compensated people on your staff, even more so than the owner if they are true rock stars. This can create friction among the troops. Support your salespeople and make sure everyone recognizes these employees are taking a risk by being in sales, assuming your sales staff's pay is based on performance (it should be). Salespeople are willing to ask people for money, a job that other staff are not always willing, or qualified, to do. As long as your pay plan is set up to compensate salespeople properly for the right actions, which can be tied to profit, customer satisfaction, and volume, never begrudge top salespeople a high paycheck or try to change their pay plan when they start to "make too much money." As long as the company grows profitably, don't grind down your salespeople's pay. Let them get rich and make sure the rest of the staff understands everyone eats when the salesperson sells. There is no room for petty jealousy. Onward and upward.

Chapter 9

EMPLOYEES

> "I like work; it fascinates me. I can sit and look at it for hours."
>
> —Jerome K. Jerome

> "Like vinegar to the teeth, and smoke to the eyes, so are the lazy to their employers."
>
> —Proverbs 10:26

This chapter is another example of me trying to cram into one short chapter a topic that libraries of books have been written about. I beg forgiveness for this and assure you, after reading hundreds of books, I get sick of reading pages and pages before I can put anything into practice or change my business today. I am ADD and need action, not philosophy. I want to move quickly and cram your brain full of actionable ideas you can implement right now. This means we can't explore most of these topics nearly as deeply as I would like to, but my goal is that after you get through a chapter, you will need to take a couple of days or weeks off to implement what you just read. You won't get as many stories, and foundation-building guidance, but that's okay. Here comes a tidal wave of actionable, moneymaking, headache-saving ideas about employees.

EMPLOYEES: THE GOOD, THE BAD, AND THE UGLY

Employees are either the most wonderful part of having a business or the bane of your existence. There is nothing like people working hard to achieve your goals and make you money while you nap on a beach in Tahiti. They become the bane of your existence because, sometimes, you find yourself paying people who screw up your business, steal from you, piss off customers, and engage in all manner of gut-wrenching activities.

I want to be totally transparent in this chapter. I have read many books that imply if you follow their 16-step system for employee management, you will never have another employee problem. While that may have been the authors' reality, I have never achieved that utopia. My commitment to you is, if you use the systems outlined in this book, you will get more production out of your people, and they will bring you a lot more joy with a lot less heartburn. That said, anytime you have employees, there will be a time and headache factor. I am here to maximize the return on your efforts and minimize your brain damage.

Before I get into the blocking and tackling of employees, and employee management, I have to refer back to chapter 4. The foundation of having and living strong core values is priceless. Living those core values out loud and obnoxiously did an amazing job of screening employees. When my core values are oozing out of every pore of every inch of my business, the people who won't fit in are turned off and never apply.

Dream employees—those who live, eat, sleep, and breathe what is important to the team—would walk through walls to get a job at my place. I had a company that built shade structures. One guy who applied to work for me included with his resume a picture of himself sitting on the street, "begging" with a cardboard sign marked, "Will work for shade."

Even when someone who is not a fit slips through the cracks, and that's a rare occurrence with a strong core-values-based culture, they quickly deselect themselves from the team. Everyone else is living the core values so strongly that these applicants don't feel they belong. How strongly your company is connected to your core values will dictate the level of benefit you get from your core values in the hiring process.

How's that for a fine little speech on the importance of corporate culture and core values? Feel free to stand up and applaud me from wherever you are reading this.

HIRING

The biggest mistake smaller businesses make—especially those with under $5,000,000 in sales—is they have lax or nonexistent hiring systems. There it is again, that pesky word *systems*. It's almost as if they are a key to this whole operation. A good hiring system has the following components:

1. A clear job description

2. A clear pay plan, tied to the exact results you want. This is another topic I could write a book on, but for now, to be clear, your people will do exactly what you pay them to do. This can be extremely helpful or painful, depending on how good your pay plan aligns with what you want them to do.

3. The minimum number of applicants you require to make a hire. Many companies just pick the "best" from whoever shows up and make a bad hire when only two to three people apply, all of whom are all subpar. I like to have at least 20 resumes and six interviews. You will have to determine these metrics for yourself. Err on the side of too many applicants and interviews. This is not the place to skimp on time and money investment.

4. An applicant attraction system, or marketing plan guaranteeing more than the minimum number of applicants. This whole system should reek of your core values to attract the right type of candidate. Don't forget to have an employee referral program. When your employees are already steeped in your culture, they have friends who will probably make good hires.

5. An interim plan for the person who will do the work while this position is being filled. There is nothing worse than having to make a hire right now. That, my friend, is a recipe for a bad hire and a lot of gray hair.

6. An interview process consisting of:

- a minimum of three interviews in three locations, only one of which can be at your office, by three different people, at three different times.
- a standardized test that ensures applicants can do the work they are hired for, with a written minimum standard of performance. It is shocking how many companies hire without a demonstration that the applicant can actually perform the work. This test would be very industry specific. Have your best technician create it for you.
- a standardized background check performed by an independent third party.
- the daily checklist they will be using when they start work

7. An on-boarding process that makes new team members feel warm, fuzzy, and loved while getting current employees fired up about welcoming them:

- Make sure the new team members' workspace, computer, phone, voicemail, e-mail is all set up, and their business cards are waiting for them. Nothing says, "You are not important" like having no business cards or e-mail.
- Throw a party and celebrate their arrival. Have some fun, and make them feel special and part of the team!
- Assign them a buddy from a different department to make sure they are assimilating well and to answer any questions they may feel are stupid and do not want to ask their boss.

- Have the first week totally planned out and action packed to get them going with some excitement. Do not set them in a room alone with six hours of reading the employee manual, watching videos, filling out paperwork, or other busywork. This is demotivating and plain lazy on the business owner's part. The first week sets the tone for what sort of company signed them on.
- Have an ongoing training program that maps out their first 30-90 days at the company, week by week, with milestones that must be met each week.
- Have another employee review process, at least quarterly, preferably monthly, to make sure everyone stays on track.

This seems like a ton of work, especially for a small business, but I have to go back to the concept of urgent and important. Hiring a warm body is urgent, while making a good hire who lasts and contributes is important. Many business owners are "too busy" running their business to take the time to set up a system to recruit, hire, and train employees. They are too busy because they don't have enough well-trained employees. If you have been in business any length of time, you know as well as I do your employees will either make or break your business and your sanity. This is one area on which you cannot skimp. Once you set up the system, it will run on autopilot with little maintenance and you can enjoy a rock-star team for years to come.

BUILDING YOUR ROCK-STAR TEAM

Let's assume you have put together a Freaking Genius hiring system and you are all staffed up. The next obvious question is "How do I lead this group of people who stare at me every day wanting to know what to do next?" As you may have guessed, the answer is a system.

I am a huge fan of checklists. My employees all knew about the checklists. There are probably a couple out there in the universe right now mocking me to other employees, imitating my voice, talking about the "importance of checklists" as other employees gather around to laugh.

As I grew my businesses, I kept bumping up against a feeling that there was too much to do, but I couldn't afford enough staff to do everything. I constantly felt that tasks fell through the cracks and important things remained unfinished. For some of these tasks, it was even unclear whose job it was to do them. This made me feel I overworked employees, added to their job descriptions, and begged them to fulfill tasks I hadn't asked them to do previously. Not fun.

Take a week and record, to the best of your ability, every single thing that gets done in your company. Pay special attention to what chores frustrate you when they are not completed or what never gets done without a fight. This is your opportunity to write down everything that would get done in a perfect world. Focus on what you have always wanted to get done but never seem to make happen. Don't forget to make note of tasks you think could be better delegated.

Once you have this list, take your time to make sure it is as complete as possible. You will break it down into two lists, in-house and contracted. One of the mistakes I made often, as a small business owner, was trying to do everything in-house, with labor I already had, "on the cheap." I recommend against that. Sub out chores such as cleaning, maintenance, changing light bulbs, and often even larger tasks that, initially, seem like things you must complete.

For example, at my car dealership, we tried forever to maintain a detail staff to keep the cars clean. It required a lot of work and was met with moderate success. When I finally paid almost double for an outside company to detail all of our cars, and another company to wash the front-line cars every week, I had the luxury of my large investment in inventory always looking tip-top. Increased sales more than paid for the extra expense, and I never had to worry about filling those low-paying positions and managing them to the standard we expected. I could focus on the moneymaking aspects of my business.

When you divide your list between in-house and contracted, don't assume a task has to be completed in-house because it has always been done in-house. If it can be subbed out, sub it out, especially if yours is a small, fast-growth company. This allows you to focus on key parts of your business and eliminate a lot of the management and headache. It also allows you to grow a lot faster. Instead of having to hire and train a legion of employees, you can run a larger company without all the overhead, headache, and risk associated with employees.

Once you have divided your list into in-house and contracted jobs, you will have to make a plan to get your contractors lined up for those jobs and then focus on the remaining in-house tasks. You will want to divide your in-house list into sensible groups. Every business has the same three main areas:

- marketing and selling your product/service
- producing/providing your product/service
- accounting for the whole mess

Once you get all of the tasks grouped into those three main areas, you should be able to put together a rough organizational chart The next step is to formalize the organizational chart with an official title and a list of duties for each position. Put your name, an employee's name, or a contractor's name under every position. Don't worry if some names are in multiple boxes, as smaller companies often have people doing multiple jobs. It is important that no jobs or tasks get left out.

THE POWER OF THE POSITION CHECKLIST

Pick whatever box you think needs the most help, and create a position checklist for that job, which will delineate exactly which tasks are to be completed on a daily, weekly, and monthly basis. Indicate the minimum standard of performance for that position. I have had the best luck when I actually did that particular job at some time in the company history and I take my experience of that job into consideration when I make the checklist. At the very least, shadow the people who perform that work as you make the checklist, especially if it involves a skilled position you are unable or unwilling to do.

As you do the job, or watch your people do the job, you will likely see that things are not being done the way you want, especially in the entry-level positions. This presents a gold mine of opportunity. People usually do things in the order they feel like doing them or follow the way a job has always been performed, rarely the most effective order. This is your opportunity, via the position checklist, to ensure every responsibility in your firm is being fulfilled in the way you want it to be and in the order you want it completed. Work once and benefit the life of your company. This is leverage at its best!

The checklist should not only have the description of tasks to be done in the correct order but also how much time tasks should take and at what time of day they should be done. That is part of the benefit of doing the job yourself while making the checklist. When something takes you ten minutes, it's hard for employees to sell you on the idea that they need an hour and one half.

Entry-level employees should have a structured list, with little employee discretion. Specific tasks should be assigned, such as "produce this," or "clean that." Their day should be broken down in 15-minute, or half-hour increments. Higher-level employees will have more general tasks, such as planning, continuing education, and meetings with subordinates. Every employee has mundane chores that need to be done every day, week, or month. There is an efficient way to do them, and a lackadaisical way to do them. For example, instead of checking and replying to e-mails every nine seconds, I usually had my employees pick two 15 minutes blocks during the day, and that was the only time they checked e-mail. Instead of going to a learning event now and then, we budgeted time for them to be at learning events.

Once it is all written down, the checklist becomes a nice overview of where you want your employees to spend time. You will be able to decide what percentage of time should be spent in each position on production, training, management, breaks, and business development.

I like to add bonus items, extra credit employees can earn but are not required to do to keep their jobs. If you don't include these, your better employees will get bored and feel unappreciated, and your average-to-poor employees will think they are doing a great job when they merely meet the minimum standard of performance. Make sure all your employees have the opportunity to show you they are ready for more responsibility and more money. This can also come in handy at employee review time.

The magic comes with the accountability piece of this pie. All employees physically check off completed tasks as they do them. At the end of the day, employees sign the sheet and go over it with their immediate supervisor. The supervisor reviews the work they have done for the day, makes sure all required tasks have been done, makes notes, including lots of praise and positive feedback when applicable, and signs the sheet. Supervisors do the same for their own checklist and review their sheet, along with all of their employees' sheets with their supervisor and so on, up the ranks to you, the owner. Every sheet has minimum standards of performance, bonus items the employees are encouraged to do, and notes from the supervisor and employee, along with the employee's and supervisor's signatures. This means you start every day with a summary of the previous day's key activities on your list, with thoughts from your employees and their supervisors about how they did. Checklists are powerful.

I met daily with my key supervisors and went over their lists and their employees' lists. To check a box indicating you completed a task when, in fact, you did not complete it was a fireable offense. Any lying, cheating, or stealing was open to instant firing in every company I have ever owned. Either all employees completed the minimum standard of performance, lied about it, and risked their job or didn't check the box.

Anytime a box wasn't checked, I had a conversation with the supervisor and we found out why. We either changed the system because we were asking too much of the employees, which was rare, or we had a conversation with the employees to find out why they didn't complete their minimum standard of performance, and we reinforced what was expected of them.

Use these checklists in the hiring, review, and firing process. When you hire applicants, go over the checklist for their job early in the process and make sure they are comfortable with what is required. Prospective employees will likely be impressed because you are far more organized and clear about what is expected of them than the other employers with whom they've interviewed.

I recommend monthly reviews for the first three months of employment and quarterly thereafter. For businesses with less than 100 employees, the owner should meet with every employee at least once per year. When you review employees and have strong use of checklists in your company, there is a lot less grey area in evaluating the employees' performance. If the checklists are all filled out, the notes are positive, and a lot of the bonus activities are completed, it is time to talk more money and responsibility. This also eliminates the low-performing employees who feel entitled to a raise. The checklists they sign, along with their supervisor's notes, give you ultimate clarity on their performance quality. Everybody is on the same page, literally.

BAD EMPLOYEES FIRE THEMSELVES

Rarely do you have to fire an employee. They fire themselves. When they are not completing the minimum standards of performance on their position checklist, they know they are not going to be able to continue at your company and wander off into the ether under their own steam.

When you do find yourself inclined to free up individuals to pursue other opportunities, it is difficult for them to claim you fired them for an illegal reason if they lied on their signed checklists and you are aware of the deception, or they have a month's worth of signed checklists stating they did not perform at the minimum level.

ROLE MODEL USE OF THE CHECKLIST

The last key to this whole checklist system is that you, first and foremost, along with your key supervisors, must publicly and obviously use your own checklist. I carried mine around with me, had it prominently displayed on my desk as I worked, and referred to it periodically. This created buy-in from the staff and buy-in for me personally, and it made it easy for me to stand firm when people did not want to use checklists.

When you have a solid system that communicates clearly and exactly what is required, you are freed up to love your employees and work on the areas of your business that you choose. Good employees love the system, because their excellent work is highlighted and recognized instead of going unnoticed. Managers love it because it makes their job so much clearer and easier. The only people who hate checklists are people who don't want to be held accountable for their results. Thank you, checklists, for helping weed those types out.

Bonus Genius: Once you have every position's checklist complete, you have the skeleton of an operations manual that you can show to investors, prospective employees, vendors, or people who want to buy your business from you. This system of position checklists, filled out with notes on progress, adds a tremendous amount of value to your business and makes it much more attractive to anyone with an interest in your company. Please hold your applause until the end of the book.

Chapter 10

CUSTOMERS: CAN'T LIVE WITH 'EM, CAN'T TAKE 'EM OUT IN THE DESERT AND BURY 'EM

"Often wrong, never in doubt."

—Mike Campion (and most likely every one of your customers)

Customers, clients, patients, donors, call 'em what you like, but they are the folks who make it all come together. This chapter is about leveraging your customers and squeezing every bit of value out of them. I recommend you read chapters 5–7 and are comfortable with their content, as most of what I am going to go over in this chapter builds on those concepts and action items.

Let's start with a twist on an old standard, our long lost friend the Pareto principle, aka the 80/20 Rule. The 80/20 Rule can be applied to your customers in a couple of interesting ways, and the first one is a slam dunk to business growth:

20 percent of your customers are responsible for 80 percent of your profits.

Don't be fooled by the simplicity of that statement. This also means 80 percent of your headache comes from 20 percent of your customers. Twenty percent of what you do in a day is responsible for 80 percent of the value you bring. The ramifications are staggering. When you look at your customer list, list your customers from most valuable to least valuable. You can slice and dice this a bunch of ways, all of which are going to bring value:

- Most total dollars spent since the beginning of time
- Most gross profit contributed since the beginning of time
- Most total dollars spent this year
- Most gross profit contributed this year
- Best referrer of valuable customers
- Most enjoyable to work with, just plain old favorites

If you haven't listed your customers like this before, you are in for a treat. Most business owners are reminded of what they already know or already suspect. Some of the revelations prove to be a complete and total shock. Now that you have the raw data, let's talk a little about what to do with it.

First, create four categories of customers. I like making fun names for them, such as Silver, Gold, Platinum, and Titanium.

If you are feeling frisky, they can be the Groupie, Sound Guy, Drummer, and Rock Star. If applicable, pick some names that are fun and industry specific. Start with your low-spending, barely-a-customer type and then work up to your Gold Bar, Triple A (not the car people), Spends-Like-Crazy customers. Since we are just talking examples, and I happen to be lazy, I am going to use A, B, C, and D for our conversation. Decide what each category's minimum and maximum spending requirements are. For example:

- A customer = $50,000+
- B customer = $25,000–$49,999
- C customer = $10,000–$24,999
- D customer = $2,000–$9,999

The reason I am having you create your categories before you look at your current customer spending is I don't want you to break down your customers and just call your top 20 percent A customers, middle 30 percent B customers, and so on. This is where you *decide* which customers you are going to attract. You might decide an A customer brings in $50,000 of gross profit per year, even though you have zero of these customers right now. This is your opportunity to be proactive and decide how your business is going to look, instead of being reactive and just figuring out how it looks now. In my example of the D customer, the value of purchases starts at $2,000 and not at $1. Decide the minimum amount of money customers need to bring in. This enables you to take excellent care of those customers and make that level of sale your cheapest offering. I always prefer taking a much lower price point for some sort of monthly or recurring income to taking a onetime purchase.

Now that you have defined the qualifications for A, B, C, and D customers, take the profit and revenue goals you set in chapter 4 and do the math to discern how many of each type of customer you will need. Always assume customers will spend the least they can in their segment. This will leave a little buffer if you don't quite get the customers you need. If your goal for next year is $1.2M, or $100K per month, using the chart above for customer values, your customer plan might look like this:

- (5) A customers ($50,000 x 5 = $250,000)
- (10) B customers ($25,000 x 10 = $250,000)
- (50) C customers ($10,000 x 50 = $500,000)
- (100) D customers ($2,000 x 100 = $200,000)
- total = $1,200,000

In this example, there are 165 customers with the top 9 percent bringing in 42 percent of the revenue. This is very typical. If this is similar to how your business breaks down, consider the D customers as loss leaders, the purpose of which is to build them into an A, B, or C sale. We will go over this in more detail later in the chapter.

CATEGORIZING YOUR CUSTOMERS WILL HELP YOU UNDERSTAND THEM

Your plan defining the number of customers you need in each category is going to be the foundation of the client acquisition program we went over in chapters 6 and 7. The next step is to understand the different types of customer you have. Many, if not most, businesses have different customers who buy different products or buy the same product for different reasons. Break these customers up into customer types so you can understand each type more clearly and communicate with them more effectively.

Let's use a church, for example, since that is a pretty generic concept most of you are familiar with. Assuming this church has 1,000 attendees, on average, it might have 200 kids in its education program, kindergarten through eighth grade, another 100 in its high school and college ministries, and 300 young families with no kids or kids in the K-8 program. Three hundred middle-aged families might have kids in the high school and college ministries, and 100 older members who are likely retired families with no kids at home. Can you see how the church would want to communicate its message to each of those segments in totally different ways?

Even within those different groups, there might be some who are visiting with a friend, some who only come at Christmas and Easter, some who come fairly regularly, and regulars who help out and volunteer. Can you see how it would make sense to communicate with these people differently as well?

You will have to decide on your customer types and group them. If you have less than three customer types, you might not be breaking them down specifically enough by criteria such as age, gender, and income. They can also be grouped by the type of product they buy, why they buy, and when they buy. If you have more than six kinds of customers, you might have to group them into larger categories or, even better, only focus on three to four of your more profitable categories. It is hard to effectively service more than six kinds of customer unless you are a larger company with complete divisions for each customer type.

Once you have broken your customers into types, it is time to come up with a good name for each. This is how you will refer to each type, internally, so the names should be descriptive. Going with our church example, young adults could be Hip Hanks, and the older folks could probably be Empty Nest Evelyns. People who only come at Christmas and Easter could be dubbed the Christmas Crowd. Ideally, you even make an avatar, or a cartoon depiction of each of these lovable customer types. The name and avatar make it immediately clear exactly what this customer type is about. The better and more specific your name, avatar, and data, the better you are going to be able to connect with and sell to them.

GET TO KNOW YOUR CUSTOMER TYPES

Now that you have them named, it is time to get to know who they are: data dump time. Start with easy demographics such as age, gender, marital status, income, and education level. Move on to what TV shows they watch, political parties they belong to, magazines they subscribe to, as well as their hobbies and travel preferences. Finally, try to get inside their head. Consider what keeps them up at night, what they love and hate, what drives them, and what makes them crazy. The goal of all of this is to be able to have two names for each customer, one based on spending level and the other based on customer type: Frustrated Frank, Happy Hanna, Cheap Charlie, and so on. You can tailor your communication and service levels to each of your customer types and spending segments (A, B, C, D).

I had a huge brain block early on in business. I thought all of my customers should get the same excellent service. The excellent part was okay, but the *same* part was dead wrong. All customers are not created equal. If any of your customers bring $150,000 in gross profit in every year, they absolutely 100 percent deserve to get the full red-carpet treatment and should have a completely different experience from that of the customer who only brings in $1,300 in profit on a onetime purchase.

Decide what an A customer should be even if you don't have any A customers now. You also get to decide what an A-customer service looks like. Go nuts here. Think of all of the amazing gifts, rewards, perks, thank-you's, surprises, extra services, freebies, and goodies that you can lavish on your A customers. Once you have that list complete, pick a subset of those benefits for your B customers. A smaller subset of your B perks go to your C customers, and once you get down to your D customers, they should be getting just your standard, but still excellent, no-frills product or service.

You can think of new and exciting services to give your A customers, as well as limiting to just your A/B customers the perks you used to give to everyone. Start to charge your C/D customers more for those perks. This is a great way to encourage your C/D customers to become more engaged with your company so they can be "promoted." Remember our friends at American Express, and the people waiting in line, hoping to get invited to pay $10,000 for the privilege of the Centurion Black card? People will pay more to be part of your A crowd.

After you have identified how many A, B, C, D customers you need—in each category—to meet your goals, and you have made an avatar for them, complete with cute name and cartoon sketch, it's time to look at the other side of the 80/20 coin: 20 percent of your customers are responsible for 80 percent of your headaches.

This is an exciting prospect when you have reliable, repeatable, scalable client acquisition systems humming along. You realize you do not need this handful of customers who are the source of the bulk of your problems. Once you come to this powerful realization, you have three options:

1. Do nothing and let these hooligans ruin your life.
2. Retrain them to be good upstanding citizens of your work universe.
3. Fire them and have a going-away party on their behalf with your staff.

Let's talk about each for a minute. If you choose option number one, you are either a masochist or need to fine-tune your client acquisition system so you are not enslaved by marginal customers.

Number two is my preferred option, but it only works if you are okay with those customers being unwilling to be retrained and leaving you. You just need to figure out why they are such a headache and address the reason. If they always want things in a rush, explain to them that from now on, there will be an up-charge. Make it big enough and you will love the extra cash when these customers want a rush service. If they constantly call, set boundaries and explain to them you are only willing to go forward if they are able to e-mail their questions no more than twice a week (or however often you feel is appropriate). If you have a group of customers who always pay late, tell them you require payment in advance or charge a late fee to make it worth the headache. The key is you get to dictate how your business life is run. Be creative and have fun with it!

Option number three is one I reserve for terrible human beings I do not want in my life. They do things such as lie, fail to pay, and verbally abuse staff, which is immediate cause for customer firing. Just call them up and tell them you will no longer be able to service their needs and wish them the best of luck in their future endeavors. It can be liberating.

UNDERSTANDING A LOSS LEADER

The last concept I want to cover in this chapter is that of loss leader. A loss leader is a free gift of value to the prospect to heighten the prospect's interest in your company and its offerings. Stick with me as this is a Freaking Genius concept that can revolutionize your business. It will look different in different businesses, depending largely on what the average ticket item is. The concept is strong and can be adapted to businesses of any size. Let's start small and work our way up.

Let's pretend you sell a $99 product or service. Many times, business owners just want to run an ad, have people give them their $99, get their product or service, and go away. That would be candy and roses, but the reality is it isn't always that easy. The gift can be a type of reward, but it needs to be related to your product or service. For a low price point such as $99, the best gifts are often information. You can offer a checklist for the "Top 10 Things You Need to Know before Buying Our Service." The information can be in the form of a free newsletter sent monthly to prospects, full of information about the benefits of adding your product or service to their life. The goal is to engage customers and pique their interest in your company and offerings, as opposed to just asking for $99 and hoping for the best. It can be extremely powerful.

Let's say that your entry-level product is $10,000. You are going to have a hard time going from "Hi, I'm Mike with Blah Blah Blah industries" to "Gimme ten grand!" This takes either highly compensated salespeople or phenomenal marketing materials combined with said highly compensated salespeople.

The way around this is to offer a much smaller, less scary way for your client to engage with your company. You could offer a daylong workshop to educate prospects on the topic, hit on the pain your prospects feel, and outline your solution. You could do a feasibility study for them or offer a half-day consultation. Break off the front end of your services and charge them for only that piece. You aren't trying to make money at this stage, although you are welcome to if the opportunity appears. You are trying to charge little enough to make it a no-brainer for the customer to sign up, but enough to cover your costs and make sure the customer sees what you have as a valuable offering.

You might only have a 20 percent closing rate for prospects interested in your $10,000 product now, but if you have another product the customer perceives as high value, costing somewhere between $500 and $1,500, you can reasonably expect a 50 percent closing ratio on the less expensive sale, and you are likely to get north of a 70 percent closing ratio on the more expensive sale. Run the numbers and you can see the overall gain.

I always offer customers the opportunity to apply to the big sale the money they invested on the loss leader. If they start to purchase with my company via my $1,500 loss leader, and my competitor and I both have a $10,000 product, they have already prepaid $1,500 with me. They are less likely to start over with my competitor. I am already set up in their system as a vendor, and they have a $1,500 credit. In their mind, I am already their provider. I can't emphasize enough how much higher my closing ratio is with people who have invested in a loss leader, compared with those to whom I try to sell a high-dollar ticket item. This technique can absolutely skyrocket your sales, especially for larger ticket item businesses.

Let's sum up so you don't forget any of the Freaking Genius ideas presented.

- Segment your customers by spending level.
- Create a plan, identifying how many customers you need at each spending level (A, B, C, D) to meet your goals.
- Combine these numbers with your client acquisition plan.
- Treat the customers who butter your bread differently (A, B) from the lower-level customers.
- Get to know your different types of customer.
- Create an avatar (name, picture, description) of each of your customer types.

- Communicate with each customer differently, based on how much that customer spends and customer type.
- Retrain or dump your headache customers.
- Create a loss leader to draw people into working with you, even though they pay a smaller amount to start.

Conclusion

ANOTHER REASON NAPOLEON HILL WAS A GENIUS AND THIS IS WHERE YOU GET PAID

"I not only use all the brains that I have, but all that I can borrow."

—Woodrow Wilson

Let's start this chapter with a bucket of ice to the face. If you read every word on every page of this book and agree with its genius but don't do a blessed thing, our little journey together was all for naught. A poor plan well executed beats the snot out of a perfect plan undone—every time. *Do something.*

For the 12 of you out there who are not familiar with Napoleon Hill, allow me the honor of introducing you. Young Napoleon was commissioned by the great Andrew Carnegie to go out into the world and find what made great men and women great.

Hill's book was published in 1937, after 25 years of research on more than 25,000 people. Hill distilled the characteristics of the achievers he studied, interviewed, and spent time with into 13 principles, the ninth of which is the power of the mastermind.

Discerning reader, you may think, "80-year-old book? Pass ..." If you go to that particular book expecting to study up on the latest and greatest path to making millions online, you will be sorely disappointed, but if you are interested in the unchanging principles of what makes men and women from all walks of life wealthy and successful, you will find a treasure trove. Bonus: The book was written in the 1930s and the way he writes just sounds cool.

The one component of the book I want to expand on here is the concept of the mastermind group. I have alluded to this concept a couple of times already in this book. I want to take a few pages to outline how important this practice is, how I have applied it in my life, and what it might look like in your life. Let's start with a definition of a mastermind group and move on to some simple examples. You may already be comfortable with the most basic examples, so we will go on to talk about mastermind groups at higher levels.

Hill's definition of a mastermind group in *Think and Grow Rich* is "coordination of knowledge and effort, in a spirit of harmony, between two or more people, for the attainment of a definite purpose."

UNDERSTANDING THE MASTERMIND

A simple example of that is the college experience. I have always held that the education you get in college is rarely used on a daily basis, but disciplining your mind to conform and perform is a skill with lifelong value. In addition, living in tight quarters with a like-minded group, in virtually the same circumstance and stage of life, builds relationships that are unlikely to be built at any other time. A Harvard graduate friend of mine regularly tells me the relationships he forged in college pay far larger dividends than the education he received or the fancy diploma on his wall. If we consider the college condition and hold it up to Hills' definition of "coordination of knowledge and effort, in a spirit of harmony, between two or more people, for the attainment of a definite purpose," I think the college life qualifies—not that I actually went to college, but I hear things…

Another simple example from my personal life is that of my friend and former "official paid coach" Carl. I met Carl through a friend of a friend in one of my mastermind groups. Look at me actually practicing what I preach! Although we ended our formal coaching agreement years ago, we remain friends. I value him as a person as well as someone who is amazing at getting the best out of people, and he seems willing to continue putting up with me—a match made in heaven. My wife and I visit Carl and his family once or twice a year, and he stays with us periodically. During one such visit a couple of years back, he took us to his business partner's cabin outside beautiful Loveland, Colorado. We absolutely fell in love with the concept of a cabin retreat. Less than a year later, we bought our cabin, which continues to be one of my family's most cherished possessions.

We went to visit Carl again, recently, and I laid some of my best business lovin' on him regarding how he could grow his business. I realized that after I sold my last business, I wanted to invest all of my time doing what I love: helping other business owners, playing with my dog Sadie, and flirting with my awesome wife. The nugget of wisdom in all this is that being involved in a mastermind group introduced me to Carl, which presented me with opportunities to help other business owners full-time. It also enabled me to buy a cabin and write this book as I sit in said cabin! Ripple effect at its finest, ladies and gentlemen!

Before I get into what big-boy mastermind groups look like, let me hit you with a couple of fun thoughts.

1. If you take the average income of your ten closest friends, you, sir, will have your income. If you want more income, hang out with people that have the financial situation that you are looking to achieve.

2. How you think is more important than what you do. Everything you do is driven by how you think. How you think is largely affected by those whom you spend time with.

3. "If you think you can, or if you think you can't, you are right," said Henry Ford. Why not spend time with people who will encourage you to think yourself wealthy?

Take a minute to digest those ideas, and then we can move on to what mastermind groups look like when properly executed. To all indignant readers out there screaming, "I am already in Toastmasters, my local chamber of commerce, and a neighborhood block watch," I say that these can be of value but are not the mastermind groups of which I speak.

I have, personally, been in some form of mastermind group much, if not all, of my business life. I have found it works best when there is a clear leader or moderator and all members of the group are equally committed. With a bunch of type A, driven people, who are used to employees and vendors giving them a pass on being late, it is easy to get into the look-how-busy-I-am mindset, in which every member thinks it is wholly appropriate to be late or even miss meetings altogether. This is not a great strategy in life and is totally unacceptable in a mastermind group setting.

Many of the mastermind groups I have been in or moderated have been committed to ground rules right off the bat. We committed to being there on time, every time. It was not unusual to have a $100-per-minute late fee, or, if someone was ten minutes late, the "honor" of buying dinner for the group. The group ensured that any dinner the latecomer bought for them became a commitment of several thousand dollars. If a member missed more than one meeting annually, that would be the end of that member's involvement in the group. Even the one miss often had to be "approved" for extreme circumstances such as the death of a close family member, a last-minute funeral on the day of our meeting, or a flight delay because of bad weather. I know this sounds really regimented, but it actually freed us up. Once we set the schedule for our meetings at the first of the year and set them in stone on our calendars, family, business partners, and employees all learned quickly that those meetings were sacred. This level of commitment is not necessary, but it will substantially raise the value of the experience.

In addition to an equal commitment level from all parties, here is a list of ideas and concepts used effectively in many of the groups that I lead or have participated in. Take the ones you like and don't send me angry e-mails about the ones you don't.

- **Confidentiality:** This is key. A confidentiality breach is the quickest way to blow up a group. Confidentiality means not sharing anything about your group members other than name, rank, and serial number, not even with your wife or household pet.

- **Gestalt protocol:** Members share experiences as opposed to giving advice. Some love it; others prefer telling everyone what to do.
- **Relationship building:** Members check in with every other member of the group near the beginning of the meeting with questions such as, "What is the best and worst thing that has happened in your life since we last met?" "What are you most and least looking forward to in your family, business, and personal life between now and when we meet next?"
- **Limited membership:** Groups are limited to only one person from each industry so there are no competition issues and sharing can be totally open.
- **Tool sharing:** Members share business tools and documents, such as employee handbooks, legal documents, policies, systems, and procedures. One member might have spent tens of thousands of dollars creating such materials and it brings tremendous value to the group. Make sure you give and not just get.
- **Educational information:** Members pass along information about the books they are reading and courses they are taking.
- **Business resources:** Members share information about resources or vendors that work and don't work.

- **Personal information:** Members share information about personal as well as business matters.
- **Uninhibited communications:** Family and business partners are not allowed in the group so communication about family and business partner issues is not inhibited.
- **Separate "spouse masterminds":** The group creates a separate mastermind group for spouses so they can get similar benefits without violating the above rule.
- **Giving "the floor":** Some or all members at each meeting have the chance to present, one at a time, an issue that could benefit from the experience and wisdom of the group.
- **Annual retreat:** Members organize a two- to three-day retreat for focused learning/growing/team building.
- **Financial commitment:** Every member makes a financial commitment to the group to encourage taking the group seriously and making it a priority. Groups I have belonged to expected contributions of $5,000–$30,000 annually, per member, depending on the level of the group.
- **Fun event:** Members organize some sort of fun activity or party with families once or twice a year.
- **Membership categories:** Some group memberships are limited to similar ages/stages in life, for example,

> members with young families, members who are all single or all over the age of 50. Some groups welcome members of all ages and stages in life. The important thing is to make this distinction at the beginning so there is no friction when adding or losing members.

If this sounds like a big commitment and a lot of work, it is, but the benefits can be life changing. Many of these well-run groups stay together and benefit for decades. I can't count the times during a mastermind group when people smarter than me told the group about a problem that they had struggled with for months or years and that the group was able to solve in one meeting. It wasn't because of my innate genius, although there's plenty of that, but rather, the perspective. As a group, because we weren't close to the problem and enmeshed in it, we could evaluate the situation from a more objective perspective.

There is something magical about getting a group of like-minded people together, all focused on one person's business or issue. It is an irreplaceable experience. I believe in this concept so passionately I actually lead a couple of mastermind groups as part of what I do for businesses, along with group coaching and one-on-one coaching. As lazy as I am and as hard pressed as I am to do things that require work, there are some things that can be accomplished only in a mastermind group. They just can't happen in any other forum. That said, I am extremely selective about whom I coach. If you think we might be a good fit, shoot me an e-mail on any of my websites, and I will let you know if I have an opening and what the application process looks like. You also should be selective, and make sure you work with a coach who gets you and speaks your language. Don't cheap out here!

This relationship should be life changing and produce at least ten times the return on your time and money investment. Don't settle for less! If you feel this is too much, go back and re-read chapter 1. Nothing will work until you do.

It makes me insane to see people come out of college at age 23, with six figures of debt, no marketable work experience, and balk at an investment in coaching, a mastermind group, courses, or a $20 book. It makes no sense for people to spend all that time and money on an education that provides very little specialized knowledge but then be unwilling to invest in information, coaching, and help that can actually make them money.

Prior to selling our car dealership, we hired a coach who worked for a consulting company. This guy cost me around $4,000 per day, depending on his travel expenses, and we used him about once every month. This sounds expensive because it was, but let me give you some of the value I got in return.

One of the benefits he offered was the ability to benchmark. We made somewhere around $250 per unit in backend profit, between warranties, GAP insurance, and the like, whereas other dealers averaged closer to $1,000. Every 100 cars we sold at our profit margin cost us $75,000 in profit. The coach helped me understand why our margins weren't where they should be and gave me data that allowed me to confront my finance manager about his performance. I got a team member in that position who could hit the numbers. The coach's market knowledge and feedback also allowed me to set expectations when hiring a finance manager, not based on my own experience and biases but on what he was reporting as standards in my industry. I could go on describing areas he helped us with. That $4,000 per day earned us many times more than we paid him. On the flip side, there were other aspects of my business that were thriving. Knowing we were already at or above average in those areas, I saved a lot of time and money not trying to improve them for limited returns, and instead, I was able to focus on the low-hanging fruit that needed fixing immediately. The confidence to know that you are on the right track goes a long way.

Books and courses have tremendous value. I have invested thousands of dollars and hours in books, tapes, CDs, seminars, courses, and the like. That said, nothing rivals the ability to ask someone who has been down that road to apply his or her specialized knowledge to your specific and current situation for real-time feedback. In addition to the raw knowledge a good coach brings, there is something special about the self-confidence gained from moving forward on a track that is proven, as opposed to just taking a bunch of swings and hoping to connect at some point.

There is no finer investment than that of investing in yourself. Everything else will age, get stolen, stop being cool, become outdated, and most likely end up in the trash heap. The money you invest in yourself will continue to pay dividends for the rest of your life unless, of course, you get hit by a car and perish tomorrow. In that case, the money was largely wasted.

On that note, let me thank you for taking this journey with me and congratulate you on now having a full tool belt with which to grow your business and free up your life. I love to hear from people who buy and read my books cover to cover. Please feel free to e-mail me anytime or come to a speaking engagement, grab me afterward, and let me know a little about your story.

To your continued success!